make your own
MEDALLION

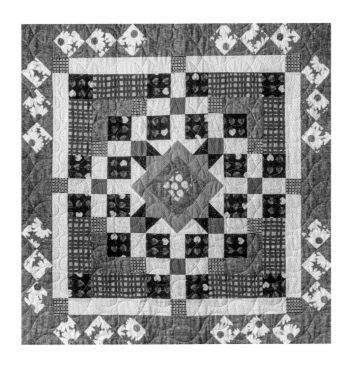

Erin Burke Harris

Published in 2017 by Lucky Spool Media, LLC
www.luckyspool.com
info@luckyspool.com

Text © Erin Burke Harris
Editor: Susanne Woods
Design: Page + Pixel
Illustrations by: Kari Vojtechovsky
  and Courtney Kyle
Photographs by: Page + Pixel

Note to copy shops: pages 130-141 may be
reprinted for personal use only.

Author photo © Marcia Seiler

9 8 7 6 5 4 3 2 1
First Edition
Printed in China

Library of Congress Cataloging-in-Publication
Data available upon request

ISBN 978 1940655 29 1

Dedicated to my mom,
who bought me a sewing machine
and made me take 7ᵗʰ grade Home Ec,
just not in that order.

Table of Contents

Introduction

The idea that evolved into this book came to me like most ideas do, in the middle of the night. On the verge of falling asleep, I decided that I should make a medallion quilt. I could envision it in my head: pieced borders, solid borders, a variety of quilt blocks in one project, a wide range of colors and fabrics. The myriad possibilities excited me!

No matter that I had never made a medallion quilt at the time. I understood the structure: a central motif surrounded by a series of borders. I had a number of quilt blocks that were one-offs—things I sewed that, for whatever reason, I couldn't imagine making dozens of for a larger quilt. So, I decided to start with one of those blocks and see if my idea had legs.

I grabbed one of my orphaned quilt blocks for a center medallion and put it up on my design wall. I thought about what I wanted for a first border and realized just how many options there were. I could add a solid piece of fabric. I could use pieced blocks around the entire perimeter or solid borders with the pieced blocks as cornerstones. And what size should the border be?

This is the part when I let you in on a little secret: Congratulations, you just bought a book about math.

Oh, wait, you thought this was about medallion quilts? Ok, it's that, too. I promise it is! As I worked on my project, it became clear to me that the key to making my own medallion quilt would be tackling the math head on. The main challenge I faced was figuring out how to make all the units and blocks fit together, border by border.

I know many people who don't enjoy math or think that they are not good at it. I am in the opposite camp. I like working with fractions and I frequently flex my multiplication and division muscles. I admit to geeking out a little bit when I figure out the geometry needed to bring my drawn designs to reality. It's just so satisfying when it all works out. I wrote this book as a guide for making your own medallion quilt, starting in the center and working out, one border at a time. You don't need to worry about the math. I did it for you. I've included 30 different quilt blocks, in three to six sizes each, so you can sew the size block you need without having to figure out how large to cut the pieces. There are six additional center medallions so you can start building your own quilt right away. I also give you tips and tricks to ensure that you finish with a successful medallion quilt. And if designing your own quilt seems daunting, you will find six medallion quilt patterns for you to sew. No extra math required.

When I finished my first medallion quilt, I knew that it would not be the last. Each border I added changed the look of the quilt and added to my excitement about the project. I had a lot of fun making that first medallion project and still enjoy mixing and matching blocks and borders to create medallion quilts from scratch. I'm looking forward to seeing how you use Make Your Own Medallion to build one-of-a-kind quilts. I'd love it if you would share photos of your work and with the larger quilting community on social media. Tag your pictures with the hashtag #makeyourownmedallion so we can all discover the creative ways **you** Make Your Own Medallion.

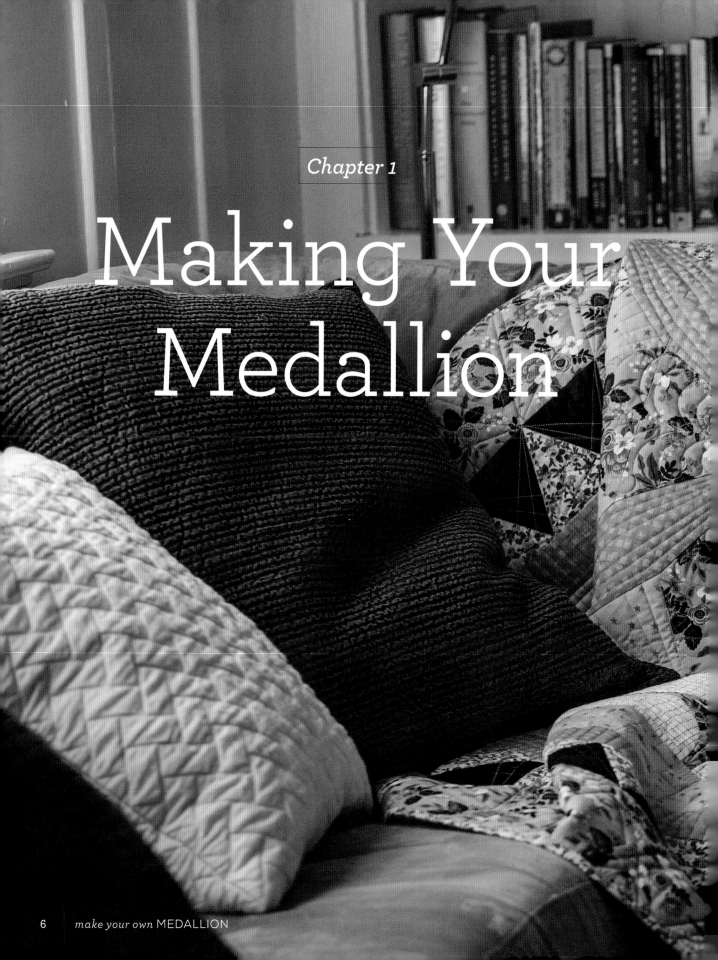

Chapter 1

Making Your Medallion

The Anatomy of a Medallion Quilt

The majority of patchwork quilts are based on a grid structure, with one block per square in the grid. The blocks are sewn together in rows of equal size and then the rows are sewn together to form the quilt top. The blocks can have sashing between them and a border surrounding them, but the main structure is a grid.

Medallion quilts are constructed differently from their block-based counterparts — they are built from the center out. Here's some information about the different components that come together to make a medallion quilt.

CENTER MEDALLION

As the focal point of your quilt, the center medallion is the star of the show. It sets the tone for the quilt and the borders that follow. There are myriad choices as to what can be used as a medallion. Something as simple as a pieced quilt block or a fabric panel can be just as effective as an intricately appliquéd or paper-pieced image. The size of the center medallion is flexible, too. It can be as small or as large as you like.

SINGLE FABRIC BORDER

Just like it sounds, a single fabric border is from just one fabric. Shorter borders are cut from the width of the fabric. Longer borders can be pieced either from two or more fabric widths or cut from the fabric's length. Choosing which method to use is a matter of personal preference. When using solid, solid-like and small-scale printed fabrics, I piece my long borders. If the border is from a larger-scale print or a pattern that will be hard to match, I prefer cutting from the length of the fabric.

BLOCK BORDERS

Sewing individual quilt blocks together to form a border is the hallmark of medallion quilts. You can choose to use one individual block, repeated again and again, or you can mix-and-match blocks in a single border. Using some pieced blocks along with the uncut squares or rectangles of fabric is another way to use blocks in borders. Borders made from blocks provide a great opportunity to play up shapes, colors and fabrics, too.

CORNERSTONES

Aptly named, the block placed in the corner where two borders meet at a right angle, is called a cornerstone. This piece of the medallion quilt can be a simple square of fabric or a pieced block. Cornerstones are a great opportunity to showcase the quilt's design elements and add contrast to a border.

Single Fabric Border

Center Medallion

Block Borders

Cornerstones

Developing a Design

Sewing a medallion quilt follows this basic formula: start with a center medallion and build the quilt out, one border at a time. As simple as that sounds, there is a little more to it than that. It's just like having a good set of blueprints when building a house.

THAT FOUR LETTER WORD: MATH

Many people don't like talking or thinking about quilt math, but it is a necessary part in planning a good medallion quilt. I designed this book with the math-shy in mind, creating multiple-sized blocks with their required measurements right at your fingertips. While all the components in this book are easy to use without requiring multiple calculations, you are going to have to do some simple math.

The finished size of your center medallion will dictate what your options are for the first border. Using a medallion with a finished size

that is a whole number and that is evenly divisible, will give you the greatest flexibility as you build your quilt. The medallions in this book are 12″, 15″, 18″, 20″, 24″ or 30″ for just this reason. They support borders that are pieced from more than one size block. Likewise, the blocks have measurements for at least three sizes between 2″ and 6″, giving you endless mix and match opportunities.

Keep this in mind as you choose the blocks and add subsequent borders to your quilt. Evenly divisible numbers work the best and give you the most options. In reality though, even numbers don't always happen. That's okay! You can always add a border of any width that is cut from a single fabric in order to make your quilt top the size you need it to be. Not only does this help even out measurements, a single fabric border can be a great design element, giving your quilt some space for your eyes to rest.

When adding borders to your quilt, it is important to remember that you are increasing the size of your quilt top on all four sides. The finished measurement of the quilt top will increase by twice the width of one border. There have been moments when I have forgotten this and ended up with a quilt top much larger than I had intended. Now I think of the size I want the quilt top to be after adding the border and then work backwards. For example, if there is a 6″ difference between my finished center medallion and the quilt top with one border, I divide 6″ in half and cut my border components so each will be 3″ when finished.

REPEAT THAT, PLEASE

A successful medallion takes design elements from the center and repeats them in the next borders. Using the same blocks, shapes, colors, fabrics or motifs as repeating elements, will give your quilt a more cohesive design.

BLOCKS AND SHAPES

When choosing blocks for a border, consider more than their size. The majority of the blocks provided in this book are squares and rectangles, but their pieces form triangles or other angled lines. Each block has its unique characteristics and still shares design elements with many of the other blocks in the book. This allows you to creatively choose from a variety of blocks to support and mimic the design elements of your center medallion.

Not everything is straight lines, though. A handful of the blocks have curves, either achieved by curved piecing or appliqué. Using these blocks to break up the angular nature of triangles and squares can work well to create visual interest in your quilt.

COLORS

One of the easiest ways to create a great medallion quilt is to pick a color palette and use it throughout the quilt. This can be choosing a simple two-color combination, like white and red, or more complicated like using all of the shades of the rainbow. Think about using only cool or warm tones as the guidelines for your palette. Choose one color like blue, but use all the shades from the lightest sky to the darkest indigo. Or pick a focal fabric that allows the colors in that print to dictate the remaining colors. In the end, an established color palette will provide natural repetition in your design.

FABRICS AND MOTIFS

Choose fabrics that have different motifs like dots, checks or flowers. Repeat these elements by using fabrics that have similar motifs, but in different scales. If one of your prints has a pink background, having that same pink in another print will create cohesiveness. Consider using one fabric in multiple places. This builds a relationship between the medallion and the borders. Adding solids or solid-like fabrics with the prints, will make the fabrics pop and give your eyes a place to rest.

SIZE MATTERS

While repetition of the medallion's design elements is important, you do not want every component to be the same scale and size. Likewise, using a variety of fabrics with prints of differing scales will enhance the design. Keep in mind that cutting up large-scale prints into small pieces doesn't always work well, because the design can get lost. These types of fabrics work best as focal prints and single fabric borders, where you can see the design in its entirety.

Cutting & Piecing for Accuracy

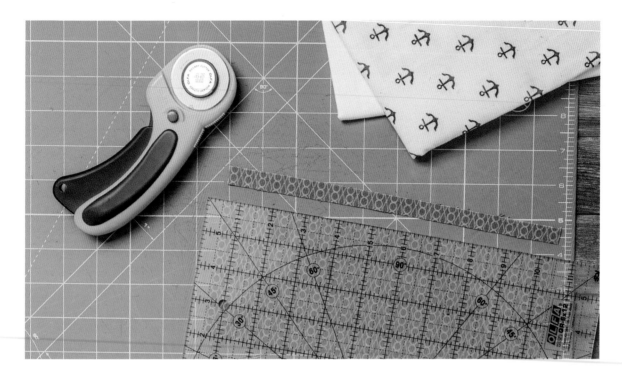

When working on a medallion quilt, accuracy in piecing is paramount. Even the smallest discrepancy multiplied over a handful of blocks can make a border shorter or longer than it should be. With a medallion quilt, an inexact border will impact each border that follows, so it is important to be accurate from the start.

SEAM ALLOWANCE

Any quilter knows that maintaining the correct seam allowance is key to achieving even edges and perfect points. All the blocks in this book use a standard quilting ¼˝ seam. Before beginning the projects, check to make sure you are sewing an accurate seam allowance. Using a ¼˝ piecing foot and marking the seam allowance with a piece of tape on your machine is helpful in keeping your seams consistent.

BLOCK CONSTRUCTION

The methods I used to construct the quilt blocks in this book were chosen because I find them to be the most consistently accurate. Many of the blocks were made using the stitch-and-flip method which involves drawing a diagonal line on a square, sewing on that line and then trimming the excess fabric away, ¼˝ from the sewn line. While there is some fabric waste with this method, it avoids sewing along stretchy bias edges, which can easily distort the shape of the block. Other blocks in the book are sewn larger and then trimmed to size. Again, consistency is the goal and having a little extra fabric to cut away is much better than ending up with a block that is too small.

MEASURING AND CUTTING BORDER BY BORDER

When I start a new quilt project, I often want to cut everything first so I can get to the good part: the sewing. With medallion quilts, though, it is advisable to cut the pieces on a border-by-border basis. This way, if your quilt top isn't measuring exactly as it should and you need to make adjustments, you won't have a pile of unusable fabric pieces staring you in the face.

The best on-going strategy for maintaining accuracy is to measure your quilt top between borders to ensure everything is progressing on track. To do this, lay the top on a flat surface and measure from edge to edge through the centers of the quilt. If the measurements are correct, carry on and cut that next border. If they aren't, determine if there is an obvious problem you can easily fix. If not, you may need to change your strategy or add a single fabric border to get the quilt top to the correct dimensions.

SEWING PIECED BORDERS

Sewing numerous blocks into pieced borders seems simple enough, but the longer the border is, the more difficult it is to maintain straight and even edges. To make this process more manageable and keep everything lined up properly, join the blocks in sets of two. Lay the blocks on a flat surface, making sure all the raw edges and seams match before pinning and then sewing them together. After pressing the seam, pin and sew two sets of blocks together in the same manner, continuing until the entire border is pieced.

ATTACHING BORDERS

To add borders, lay the quilt top right side up on a flat surface with the border face down on top of it. Fold the border in half to find its center and match this to the center of the quilt top's edge. Lining up the raw edges and seam lines (if applicable), match the ends of the border to the quilt top's edges and pin the border in place, easing any excess fabric. The left and right side borders are attached first and then top and bottom borders are sewn on next.

PRESSING

A well-pressed block helps with accuracy too. Using a good, hot iron is necessary to get seams to lay flat. Other than that, most pressing decisions are a matter of personal preference. I like to use steam when pressing, but spray starch is a good alternative. Most of the time I do not call out whether a seam should be pressed open or to the side. When I do though, it's because it matters. For example, when adding a pieced border to a single fabric border, always press towards the single fabric border because everything lays flatter. When paper piecing, seams may be pressed open because they can be bulky. If the one fabric is noticeably lighter in color than the other, press towards the darker fabric. Beyond that, I recommend looking at the way the block seams will meet and interact and make your pressing decision based on the method that will give you the flattest possible intersection.

My Favorite Tools

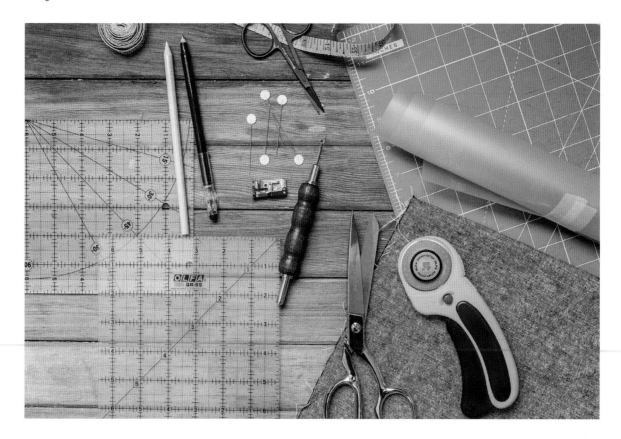

Beyond a sewing machine, fabric and thread, there are a few tools that will make sewing the projects in this book easier and more enjoyable.

¼″ PIECING FOOT

This presser foot, sometimes called a piecing foot or patchwork foot, is especially helpful in ensuring accurate ¼″ seams.

CUTTING TOOLS

Fabric scissors, a rotary cutter with a sharp blade and a self-healing mat are essential. I also have a pair of paper scissors close at hand to use when cutting templates and foundation paper piecing patterns. My small embroidery scissors are used to snip threads and chain-pieced blocks. They also come in handy for clipping fabric when I appliqué.

RULERS

While I wish one ruler would fit all, I find that having various sizes at hand is most helpful. No sewing room is complete without a 6″ × 24″ ruler. I use mine for cutting along the folded width of the fabric. My 6″ × 12″ ruler may be my favorite. I use it to sub-cut longer widths of fabric and while working on small blocks. Additionally, a 6½″ square ruler is the perfect size for trimming any of the individual blocks included in this book.

MEASURING TAPE

As you build your medallion quilt, it will quickly outgrow your quilting ruler. Use a long, flexible measuring tape to check the dimensions of your quilt top as you sew.

PINS

I'm picky when it comes to the pins I use. For piecing, I like Clover patchwork and quilting pins. They are thin, long, sharp and have glass heads that won't melt if you accidentally run over them with your iron. I also use small appliqué pins to keep my fabric pieces secure while I baste them.

STITCH RIPPER

Mistakes happen. Need I say more?

SEAM GUIDE

This handy tool is great for checking the accuracy of seam allowances. It is also useful when you need to add a seam allowance to a template or have to press something under at a particular measurement.

MARKING TOOLS

Many of the blocks require you to draw a diagonal line on the fabric as a stitching guide. There are also some blocks that require you to trace a template onto fabric. In both of these instances, I like using a sharp pencil or a Frixion pen on light to medium hued fabrics. For darker fabrics, I have a white chalk pencil that works well. A fine-tipped permanent marker is great for tracing templates onto template plastic.

TEMPLATE PLASTIC

Some of the blocks and medallions require you to cut fabric pieces using templates. I like using clear template plastic because it makes the template long-lasting and durable. Place the template plastic over the printed template and trace the cutting lines with a fine tip, permanent marker. Transfer any additional markings to the template and then cut it out from the plastic. You can then use the template to trace the shape directly onto the fabric.

PAPER

When foundation paper piecing, I use plain 20lb. copy paper as my foundation. It's lightweight, easy to tear and widely available. I always have some heavier card stock on hand for the times I need a quick, one-off template or for making circles using the aluminum foil appliqué method used in the medallion on page 110.

DESIGN WALL

I love having a flannel design wall to use as I make my quilts. It is so helpful to me to be able to see how my design is progressing as I sew, and to be able to step back for a different view. I understand that not everyone has the space or the inclination to have a dedicated design wall. In that event, I recommend covering some lightweight foam boards in batting or flannel, so that you can prop them up against the wall when you need them. If they aren't needed, store them in a closet or under a bed. You can even store your in-progress projects on the boards, taking them out when you are ready to work on them again.

CAMERA

My smart phone's camera is among my most-used quilting tools. I snap photos of objects, shapes and places that inspire me. I also take pictures of my quilts as I am working on them. It is so useful to have a visual reminder of how I laid a quilt out if I need to step away before finishing. The built-in editing functions are handy, too. I use them to turn the photos to black and white, to check the contrast in my fabrics. Sometimes I use the crop function to see what parts of the quilt are working well together, and isolate those that aren't.

Inspired to Get Started?

Great! Each of the quilts shown on these two pages has a stand-alone pattern that can be found in Chapter 4. So, if you are anxious to get sewing, jump right in and make one of the quilts just as I have designed it.

If you like one of these settings, but think you might want to adjust some of the border blocks, go for it! Because I designed this book with mixing and matching in mind, I've made it easy to keep the structure, but change the blocks to suit your unique vision, border by border. This allows you to modify the look of the quilt to tailor it to your individual taste, without having to do any of the math to ensure a perfect fit for your blocks. Simply consult the quilt pattern to see what size block is required for the border you want to change, then substitute it with any of the same-sized finished blocks using the handy charts in Chapter 2. It's that easy.

The center medallions can also be changed! Choose one of the six from Chapter 3, one of the six from Chapter 4 or substitute one of your favorites that finishes to the same size as the one in the pattern. If your chosen center is a little smaller than the pattern states, you can easily add an additional solid or pieced border to make it a perfect fit.

The tools and the math for swapping blocks and building borders are at your fingertips just waiting for your own inspiration. So, gather some fabrics, start cutting and get sewing! With 30 blocks, 12 medallions and 6 quilt schematics...the possibilities for creating your own custom medallion quilt are endless!

Chapter 2

The Blocks

make your own MEDALLION

Block 1 | # Half-Square Triangle *Makes 2 Units*

1. On the wrong side of the Fabric A square, draw a diagonal line from corner to corner.

2. Place the Fabric A square right sides together with the Fabric B square. With the raw edges matching, sew ¼″ from each side of the drawn line.

3. Using a rotary cutter and ruler, cut the block diagonally on the drawn line.

4. Press the units open and trim to size.

FINISHED BLOCK SIZE	CUT FABRIC A	CUT FABRIC B	TRIM SEWN UNIT TO
2″ × 2″	(1) 3¼″ × 3¼″	(1) 3¼″ × 3¼″	2½″ × 2½″
3″ × 3″	(1) 4¼″ × 4¼″	(1) 4¼″ × 4¼″	3½″ × 3½″
4″ × 4″	(1) 5¼″ × 5¼″	(1) 5¼″ × 5¼″	4½″ × 4½″
4½″ × 4½″	(1) 5¾″ × 5¾″	(1) 5¾″ × 5¾″	5″ × 5″
5″ × 5″	(1) 6¼″ × 6¼″	(1) 6¼″ × 6¼″	5½″ × 5½″
6″ × 6″	(1) 7¼″ × 7¼″	(1) 7¼″ × 7¼″	6½″ × 6½″

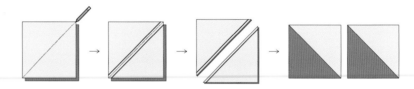

Block 2 | Flying Geese *Makes 1 Unit*

1. Draw a diagonal line from corner to corner on the wrong side of both Fabric B squares.

2. Place 1 marked square on top of the Fabric A rectangle, right sides together and matching the raw edges. Sew on the drawn line. Trim the corner ¼″ from the stitching and press.

3. Repeat Step 2 sewing the second Fabric B square on the opposite end of the Fabric A rectangle and press.

FINISHED BLOCK SIZE	CUT FABRIC A	CUT FABRIC B	UNFINISHED UNIT WILL BE
1″ × 2″	(1) 1½″ × 2½″	(2) 1½″ × 1½″	1½″ × 2½″
1½″ × 3″	(1) 2″ × 3½″	(2) 2″ × 2″	2″ × 3½″
2″ × 4″	(1) 2½″ × 4½″	(2) 2½″ × 2½″	2½″ × 4½″
2½″ × 5″	(1) 3″ × 5½″	(2) 3″ × 3″	3″ × 5½″
3″ × 6″	(1) 3½″ × 6½″	(2) 3½″ × 3½″	3½″ × 6½″

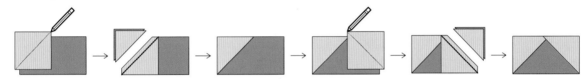

Block 3 | # Quarter-Square Triangle *Makes 2 Units*

FINISHED BLOCK SIZE	CUT FABRIC A	CUT FABRIC B	TRIM SEWN UNIT TO
2" × 2"	(1) 3¼" × 3¼"	(1) 3¼" × 3¼"	2½" × 2½"
3" × 3"	(1) 4¼" × 4¼"	(1) 4¼" × 4¼"	3½" × 3½"
4" × 4"	(1) 5¼" × 5¼"	(1) 5¼" × 5¼"	4½" × 4½"
4½" × 4½"	(1) 5¾" × 5¾"	(1) 5¾" × 5¾"	5" × 5"
5" × 5"	(1) 6¼" × 6¼"	(1) 6¼" × 6¼"	5½" × 5½"
6" × 6"	(1) 7¼" × 7¼"	(1) 7¼" × 7¼"	6½" × 6½"

1. Sew the 2 Fabric A and B squares together following the instructions for Half-Square Triangles (see page 20). Do not trim.

2. On the wrong side of 1 HST unit, draw a diagonal line from corner to corner, perpendicular to the seam.

3. Place the 2 HST units right sides together with the seams and raw edges matching, making sure that opposite fabrics are facing. Sew ¼" from each side of the drawn line.

4. Using a rotary cutter and ruler, cut the block diagonally on the drawn line.

5. Press the units open and trim to size.

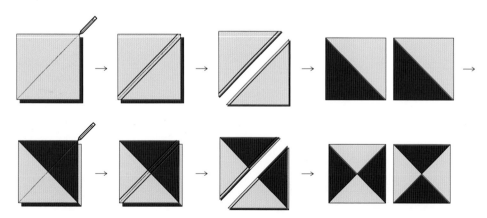

Half-Rectangle Triangle

Makes 2 Units

FINISHED BLOCK SIZE	CUT FABRIC A	CUT FABRIC B	TRIM SEWN UNIT TO
1½″ × 3″	(1) 2½″ × 5″	(1) 2½″ × 5″	2″ × 3½″
2″ × 4″	(1) 3″ × 6″	(1) 3″ × 6″	2½″ × 4½″
2½″ × 5″	(1) 3½″ × 7″	(1) 3½″ × 7″	3″ × 5½″
3″ × 6″	(1) 4″ × 8″	(1) 4″ × 8″	3½″ × 6½″

1. Cut both rectangles diagonally from corner to corner.

LEFT-LEANING HRTS
For left-leaning HRTs, cut from the bottom right to the top left (top).

RIGHT-LEANING HRTS
For right-leaning HRTs, cut from the bottom left to the top right (bottom).

2. With the right sides facing, pin the half-rectangle triangles together along the diagonal edge. The tips of the triangles will extend ¼″ beyond the edges.

3. Sew the triangles together, open and press.

LEFT-LEANING HRTS
To trim the units to size, place the ruler on the block so that the seam line runs through the point on the ruler that is ¼″ in from the top and left edge of the 'trim sewn unit to' size. Trim along the right edge and the top.

RIGHT-LEANING HRTS
To trim the units to size, place the ruler so that the seam line runs through the point on the ruler that is ¼″ in from the top and right edge of the 'trim sewn unit to' size. Trim along the right edge and the top.

4. Rotate the block 180 degrees and line up the trimmed sides with the 'trim sewn unit to' size. Trim the remaining 2 sides.

5. Repeat with the remaining 2 triangles.

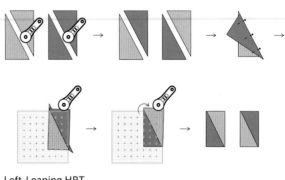

Left-Leaning HRT

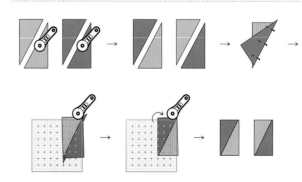

Right-Leaning HRT

Block 5 | # 4-Patch *Makes 1 Unit*

1. Sew one Fabric A square to each Fabric B square. Press the seams in the same direction.

2. Sew the 2 pairs together with the opposite fabrics facing. Press.

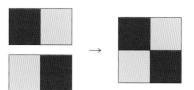

FINISHED BLOCK SIZE	CUT FABRIC A	CUT FABRIC B	UNFINISHED UNIT WILL BE
2″ × 2″	(2) 1½″ × 1½″	(2) 1½″ × 1½″	2½″ × 2½″
3″ × 3″	(2) 2″ × 2″	(2) 2″ × 2″	3½″ × 3½″
4″ × 4″	(2) 2½″ × 2½″	(2) 2½″ × 2½″	4½″ × 4½″
4½″ × 4½″	(2) 2¾″ × 2¾″	(2) 2¾″ × 2¾″	5″ × 5″
5″ × 5″	(2) 3″ × 3″	(2) 3″ × 3″	5½″ × 5½″
6″ × 6″	(2) 3½″ × 3½″	(2) 3½″ × 3½″	6½″ × 6½″

Block 6 | # 9-Patch   *Makes 1 Unit*

1. Sew 3 Fabric A squares to the 3 Fabric B squares. Press the seams towards Fabric A.

2. Sew the remaining Fabric B square to the Fabric A side of a pair of squares. Press the seam towards Fabric A. Set aside.

3. Sew a Fabric A square to the Fabric B side of each of the remaining 2 pairs of squares. Press the seams towards Fabric A.

4. Sew the 3 rows together to form the block. Press.

FINISHED BLOCK SIZE	CUT FABRIC A	CUT FABRIC B	UNFINISHED UNIT WILL BE
3″ × 3″	(5) 1½″ × 1½″	(4) 1½″ × 1½″	3½″ × 3½″
4½″ × 4½″	(5) 2″ × 2″	(4) 2″ × 2″	5″ × 5″
6″ × 6″	(5) 2½″ × 2½″	(4) 2½″ × 2½″	6½″ × 6½″

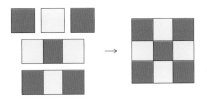

Block 7 | # Churn Dash   *Makes 1 Unit*

FINISHED BLOCK SIZE	CUT FABRIC A	CUT FABRIC B	TRIM SEWN UNIT TO
3″ × 3″			
Half-Square Triangles	(2) 2″ × 2″	(2) 2″ × 2″	(4) 1½″ × 1½″
Strip set	(1) 1″ × 6″	(1) 1″ × 6″	(4) 1½″ × 1½″
Center	(1) 1½″ × 1½″		
4½″ × 4½″			
Half-Square Triangles	(2) 2½″ × 2½″	(2) 2½″ × 2½″	(4) 2″ × 2″
Strip set	(1) 1¼″ × 8″	(1) 1¼″ × 8″	(4) 2″ × 2″
Center	(1) 2″ × 2″		
6″ × 6″			
Half-Square Triangles	(2) 3″ × 3″	(2) 3″ × 3″	(4) 2½″ × 2½″
Strip set	(1) 1½″ × 10″	(1) 1½″ × 10″	(4) 2½″ × 2½″
Center	(1) 2½″ × 2½″		

1. Make 4 Half-Square Triangle units (see page 20) using the 2 larger Fabric A squares and the 2 Fabric B squares.

2. Sew the long sides of the Fabric A and Fabric B rectangles together to form a strip set. Press. Cut the strip set into 4 equal units.

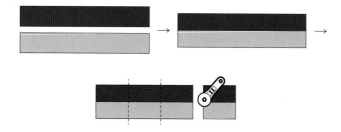

3. Arrange the block as indicated in the illustration adjacent. Sew the pieces into a 9-patch and assemble accordingly. Press the seams away from the strip set units so that the rows nest.

4. Sew the three rows into a block. Press.

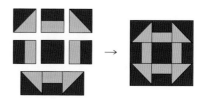

Block 8 | # Rails   *Makes 1 Unit*

1. Sew the long side of a Fabric A rectangle to the Fabric B rectangle to form a strip set. Press.

2. Sew the remaining Fabric A strip to the Fabric B side of the strip set. Press.

tip | The rails block can be strip pieced. The length of your rectangles is dependent on the number of blocks you need but the width won't change. To calculate the length, multiply the number of blocks by the length of the unfinished unit. Add 1" to allow trimming on the ends.

FINISHED BLOCK SIZE	CUT FABRIC A	CUT FABRIC B	TRIM SEWN UNIT TO
3″ × 3″	(2) 1½″ × 3½″	(1) 1½″ × 3½″	3½″ × 3½″
4½″ × 4½″	(2) 2″ × 5″	(1) 2″ × 5″	5″ × 5″
6″ × 6″	(2) 2½″ × 6½″	(1) 2½″ × 6½″	6½″ × 6½″

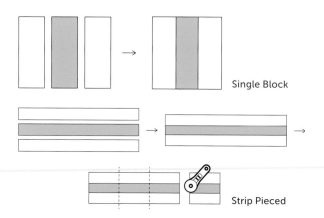

Single Block

Strip Pieced

Block 9 | **Plus** *Makes 1 Unit*

1. Sew a Fabric B square to the opposite ends of each Fabric A square. Press the seams towards the center.

2. Sew a pieced unit from Step 1 to each long side of the Fabric A rectangle. Press the seams towards the center.

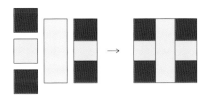

FINISHED BLOCK SIZE	CUT FABRIC A	CUT FABRIC B	UNFINISHED UNIT WILL BE
3″ × 3″			3½″ × 3½″
	(2) 1½″ × 1½″	(4) 1½″ × 1½″	
	(1) 1½″ × 3½″		
4½″ × 4½″			5″ × 5″
	(2) 2″ × 2″	(4) 2″ × 2″	
	(1) 2″ × 5″		
6″ × 6″			6½″ × 6½″
	(2) 2½″ × 2½″	(4) 2½″ × 2½″	
	(1) 2½″ × 6½″		

Drunkard's Path

Makes 1 Unit

FINISHED BLOCK SIZE	CUT FABRIC A	CUT FABRIC B	UNFINISHED UNIT WILL BE
3″ × 3″	(1) Template A 3″	(1) Template B 3″	3½″ × 3½″
4″ × 4″	(1) Template A 4″	(1) Template B 4″	4½″ × 4½″
4½″ × 4½″	(1) Template A 4½″	(1) Template B 4½″	5″ × 5″
5″ × 5″	(1) Template A 5″	(1) Template B 5″	5½″ × 5½″
6″ × 6″	(1) Template A 6″	(1) Template B 6″	6½″ × 6½″

1. Fold the quarter circle (Drunkard's Path, Template A, see page 132) in half, right sides together. Finger press the fold on the curved edge to mark the center.

2. Fold the quarter arch (Drunkard's Path, Template B, see page 130) in half, right sides together, matching the straight edges and ends. Finger press the fold at the inner edge of the arch to mark the center.

3. With the right sides together and matching the raw edges, pin the finger pressed center marks together. Pin each quarter arch side-edge to the corresponding quarter circle side-edge. Ease the fabric between the center and the sides, pinning in place.

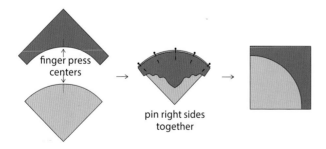

finger press centers

pin right sides together

4. Sew together, removing pins as you come to them.

5. Press the seam carefully to avoid distortion.

| # Equal-ish Triangles *Makes 1 Unit*

FINISHED BLOCK SIZE	CUT FABRIC A	CUT FABRIC B*	UNFINISHED UNIT WILL BE
2″ × 2″	(2) 2½″ × 1½″	2½″ × 2½″	2½″ × 2½″
3″ × 3″	(2) 3½″ × 2″	3½″ × 3½″	3½″ × 3½″
4″ × 4″	(2) 4½″ × 2½″	4½″ × 4½″	4½″ × 4½″
4½″ × 4½″	(2) 5 ″x 2¾″	5 ″ × 5″	5″ × 5″
5″ × 5″	(2) 5½″ × 3 ″	5½″ × 5½″	5½″ × 5½″
6″ × 6″	(2) 6½″ × 3½″	6½″ × 6½″	6½″ × 6½″

When using multiple triangles from a single fabric, cut them from a long strip instead of individual squares.

1. Sew a Fabric A side triangle (Equal-ish Triangle, Template B, see page 133) to a Fabric B triangle (Equal-ish Triangle, Template A, see page 133). Press the seam towards the darker fabric.

2. Sew a Fabric A triangle (Template A) to the other side of the Fabric B triangle. Press. Or, if you are creating a longer triangle border, sew another full triangle (Template B) to the existing full triangle piece.

3. Continue adding triangles in this manner until the desired length of the border is reached. End the border with a side triangle.

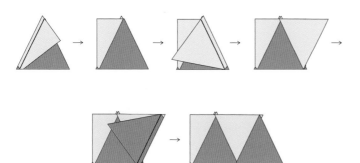

Block 12 | # Dot *Makes 1 Unit*

1. Sew a Fabric B square to 2 opposite sides of the Fabric A square. Press the seams away from the center.

2. Sew a Fabric B rectangle to each long side of the pieced unit from Step 1. Press the seams away from the center.

FINISHED BLOCK SIZE	CUT FABRIC A	CUT FABRIC B	UNFINISHED UNIT WILL BE
3″ × 3″			3½″ × 3½″
	(1) 1½″ × 1½″	(2) 1½″ × 1½″	
		(2) 1½″ × 3½″	
4½″ × 4½″			5″ × 5″
	(1) 2″ × 2″	(2) 2″ × 2″	
		(2) 2″ × 5″	
6″ × 6″			6½″ × 6½″
	(1) 2½″ × 2½″	(2) 2½″ × 2½″	
		(2) 2½″ × 6½″	

Block 13 | Square-in-a-Square *Makes 1 Unit*

1. On the wrong side of 4 Fabric B squares, draw a diagonal line from corner to corner.

2. With the right sides together, place 2 Fabric B squares on opposite sides of the Fabric A square, matching the raw edges and ensuring that the drawn line runs from the center of two sides of the Fabric A square. Sew on the drawn line. Trim the corner ¼" from the sewn line. Press the seams towards the dark fabric or open.

3. Repeat Step 2 for the remaining corners of the Fabric A square.

FINISHED BLOCK SIZE	CUT FABRIC A	CUT FABRIC B	UNFINISHED UNIT WILL BE
2" × 2"	(1) 2½" × 2½"	(4) 1½" × 1½"	2½" × 2½"
3" × 3"	(1) 3½" × 3½"	(4) 2" × 2"	3½" × 3½"
4" × 4"	(1) 4½" × 4½"	(4) 2½" × 2½"	4½" × 4½"
4½" × 4½"	(1) 5" × 5"	(4) 2¾" × 2¾"	5" × 5"
5" × 5"	(1) 5½" × 5½"	(4) 3" × 3"	5½" × 5½"
6" × 6"	(1) 6½" × 6½"	(4) 3½" × 3½"	6½" × 6½"

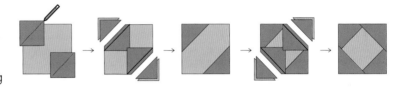

Block 14 | Cog *Makes 1 Unit*

1. Make 4 Half-Square Triangle units using the 2 Fabric A squares and the 2 Fabric B squares (see page 20).

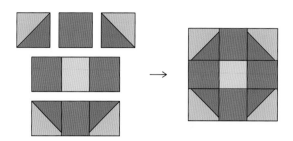

2. Arrange and sew the HST units and remaining squares into a 9-patch and press.

FINISHED BLOCK SIZE	CUT FABRIC A	CUT FABRIC B	CUT FABRIC C	CUT FABRIC D	UNFINISHED UNIT WILL BE
3″ × 3″	(2) 2″ × 2″	(2) 2″ × 2″	(4) 1½″ × 1½″	(1) 1½″ × 1½″	3½″ × 3½″
4½″ × 4½″	(2) 2½″ × 2½″	(2) 2½″ × 2½″	(4) 2″ × 2″	(1) 2″ × 2″	5″ × 5″
6″ × 6″	(2) 3″ × 3″	(2) 3″ × 3″	(4) 2½″ × 2½″	(1) 2½″ × 2½″	6½″ × 6½″

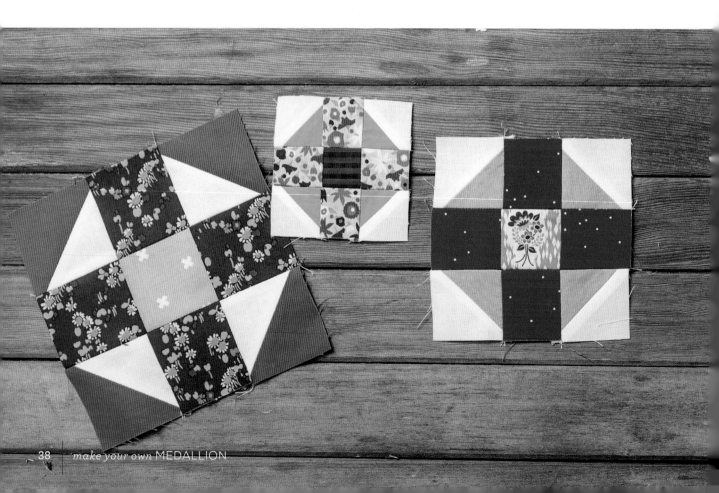

Block 15 | # Kite *Makes 1 Unit*

1. Copy the Kite foundation pattern (see page 136) at the appropriate size for your project.

2. Foundation paper piece (see page 129) the block, leaving a ¼˝ seam allowance around the outside edges.

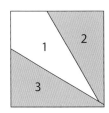

FINISHED BLOCK SIZE	FABRIC A	FABRIC B	TRIM SEWN UNIT TO
2˝ × 2˝	(2) 1¾˝ × 3½˝	(1) 1¾˝ × 4˝	2½˝ × 2½˝
3˝ × 3˝	(2) 2½˝ × 4½˝	(1) 2½˝ × 5½˝	3½˝ × 3½˝
4˝ × 4˝	(2) 3¼˝ × 5½˝	(1) 3½˝ × 6¾˝	4½˝ × 4½˝
4½˝ × 4½˝	(2) 3½˝ × 6¼˝	(1) 3½˝ × 7½˝	5˝ × 5˝
5˝ × 5˝	(2) 3¾˝ × 7˝	(1) 4˝ × 8¼˝	5½˝ × 5½˝
6˝ × 6˝	(2) 4˝ × 8¼˝	(1) 4½˝ × 9½˝	6½˝ × 6½˝

| Kite Variation *Makes 1 Unit*

1. Copy the Kite Variation foundation pattern (see page 134) at the appropriate size for your project.

2. Foundation paper piece (see page 129) the block, leaving a ¼˝ seam allowance around the outside edges.

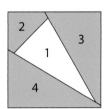

FINISHED BLOCK SIZE	FABRIC A	FABRIC B	TRIM SEWN UNIT TO
2˝ × 2˝			2½˝ × 2½˝
	(2) 1¾˝ × 3½˝	(1) 1¾˝ × 3½˝	
	(1) 2½˝ × 1½˝		
3˝ × 3˝			3½˝ × 3½˝
	(2) 2½˝ × 4½˝	(1) 2½˝ × 4½˝	
	(1) 3¼˝ × 1¾˝		
4˝ × 4˝			4½˝ × 4½˝
	(2) 3¼˝ × 5½˝	(1) 3½˝ × 5½˝	
	(1) 3¾˝ × 2¼˝		
4½˝ × 4½˝			5˝ × 5˝
	(2) 3½˝ × 6¼˝	(1) 3½˝ × 6¼˝	
	(1) 4˝ × 2½˝		
5˝ × 5˝			5½˝ × 5½˝
	(2) 3¾˝ × 7˝	(1) 4˝ × 6¾˝	
	(1) 4½˝ × 2½˝		
6˝ × 6˝			6½˝ × 6½˝
	(2) 4˝ × 8¼˝	(1) 4½˝ × 8˝	
	(1) 5˝ × 2¾˝		

Block 17 | Tulip *Makes 1 Unit*

1. Make 2 Half-Square Triangles (see page 20) with the largest Fabric A and Fabric B squares.

2. Sew the smallest Fabric B square to the Fabric C square to form a rectangle. Sew this unit to the Fabric B rectangle. Press the seams to the side.

3. Sew the 3 units and the remaining Fabric A square together to form 2 rows. Press the seams in opposite directions. Sew the rows together to complete the block.

FINISHED BLOCK SIZE	FABRIC A	FABRIC B	FABRIC C	TRIM SEWN A/B UNIT TO
4″ × 4″				(2) 2½″ × 2½″
	(1) 2½″ × 2½″	(1) 3″ × 3″	(1) 1½″ × 1½″	
	(1) 3″ × 3″	(1) 1½″ × 2½″		
		(1) 1½″ × 1½″		
5″ × 5″				(2) 3″ × 3″
	(1) 3″ × 3″	(1) 3½″ × 3½″	(1) 1¾″ × 1¾″	
	(1) 3½″ × 3½″	(1) 1¾″ × 3″		
		(1) 1¾″ × 1¾″		
6″ × 6″				(2) 3½″ × 3½″
	(1) 3½″ × 3½″	(1) 4″ × 4″	(1) 2″ × 2″	
	(1) 4″ × 4″	(1) 2″ × 3½″		
		(1) 2″ × 2″		

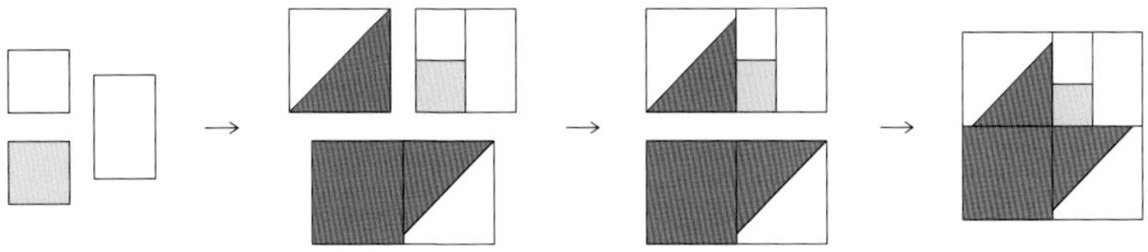

Block 18 | Chisel *Makes 1 Unit*

FINISHED BLOCK SIZE	CUT FABRIC A	CUT FABRIC B	UNFINISHED UNIT WILL BE
1″ × 2″	(1) 1½″ × 2½″	(1) 1½″ × 1½″	1½″ × 2½″
1½″ × 3″	(1) 2″ × 3½″	(1) 2″ × 2″	2″ × 3½″
2″ × 4″	(1) 2½″ × 4½″	(1) 2½″ × 2½″	2½″ × 4½″
2½″ × 5″	(1) 3″ × 5½″	(1) 3″ × 3″	3″ × 5½″
3″ × 6″	(1) 3½″ × 6½″	(1) 3½″ × 3½″	3½″ × 6½″

1. Draw a diagonal line from corner to corner on the wrong side of the Fabric B square.

LEFT-LEANING CHISEL

For a left-leaning Chisel, place the marked square on top of the Fabric A rectangle, right sides together, matching the raw edges and with the drawn line starting in the top left corner.

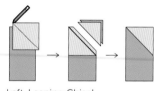

Left-Leaning Chisel

RIGHT-LEANING CHISEL

For a right-leaning Chisel, place the marked square on top of the Fabric A rectangle, right sides together, matching the raw edges and with the drawn line starting in the top right corner.

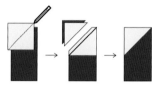

Right-Leaning Chisel

2. Sew on the drawn line. Trim the corner ¼″ from the stitching and press.

Block 19 | **X Block** *Makes 1 Unit*

FINISHED BLOCK SIZE	FABRIC A	FABRIC B	CENTER TRIMMING POINT	TRIM SEWN UNIT TO
3″ × 3″	(1) 3½″ × 3½″	(2) 1¼″ × 5¼″	1¾″	3½″ × 3½″
4″ × 4″	(1) 4½″ × 4½″	(2) 1¼″ × 7″	2¼″	4½″ × 4½″
4½″ × 4½″	(1) 4½″ × 4½″	(2) 1½″ × 7½″	2½″	5″ × 5″
5″ × 5″	(1) 5½″ × 5½″	(2) 1½″ × 8¼″	2¾″	5½″ × 5½″
6″ × 6″	(1) 6½″ × 6½″	(2) 1½″ × 10″	3¼″	6½″ × 6½″

1. Cut the Fabric A square in half along the diagonal to yield 2 triangles.

2. With the right sides together, center 1 Fabric B strip along the diagonal edge of 1 triangle. The ends of the strip will extend past the tips of the triangle. Sew in place and press the seam towards Fabric B.

3. Place the second triangle on the opposite edge of the same Fabric B strip, right sides facing. Take care that the outer tips of the triangles line up. Sew the triangle in place and press the seams towards Fabric B.

4. Using a ruler and rotary cutter, cut the unit in half along the opposite diagonal to create 2 pieced triangles.

5. Repeat Steps 2 and 3 with the remaining Fabric B strip and the 2 pieced triangles.

6. To trim the units to size, position the ruler so that the ruler lines for the center trimming point measurement (see chart above) aligns with the inner points of the triangle, both vertically and horizontally. Trim along the side and top. Rotate the block 180 degrees, realign the ruler lines and trim the remaining 2 sides.

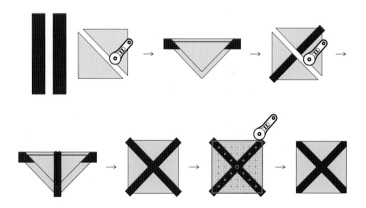

Block 20 | Peel *Makes 1 Unit*

FINISHED BLOCK SIZE	FABRIC A	FABRIC B	UNFINISHED UNIT WILL BE
2″ × 2″	(1) 2½″ × 2½″	(1) 2″ × 3½″	2½″ × 2½″
3″ × 3″	(1) 3½″ × 3½″	(1) 2¼″ × 4½″	3½″ × 3½″
4″ × 4″	(1) 4½″ × 4½″	(1) 3″ × 5¾″	4½″ × 4½″
4½″ × 4½″	(1) 5″ × 5″	(1) 3¼″ × 6½″	5″ × 5″
5″ × 5″	(1) 5½″ × 5½″	(1) 3½″ × 7″	5½″ × 5½″
6″ × 6″	(1) 6½″ × 6½″	(1) 4″ × 8¼″	6½″ × 6½″

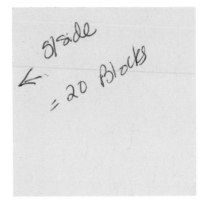

(handwritten note) 5/side ← = 20 Blocks

1. Determine which style of appliqué (see page 128) you will use and prepare the Peel Template (see page 134) and Fabric B accordingly. Cut the Peel from the Fabric B rectangle.

2. Fold the Fabric A square in half on the diagonal and the Fabric B Peel in half lengthwise and make a crease.

3. Using the creases as guides, align the Fabric B Peel on top of the Fabric A square so that the Peel shape in centered on the Fabric A square. Fuse, pin or baste in place.

4. Appliqué using your preferred method.

  → →

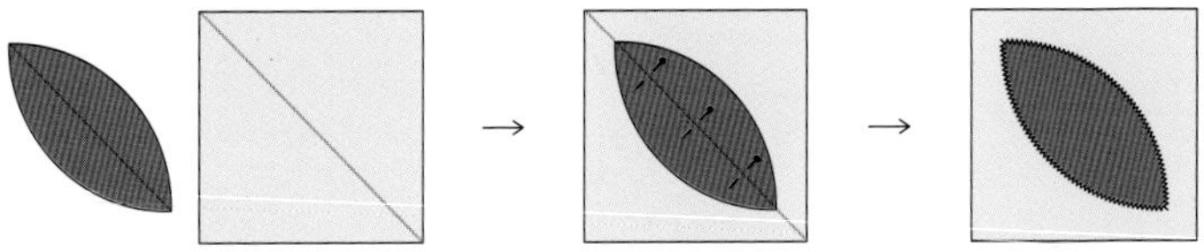

Block 21 | Diagonal Dash *Makes 1 Unit*

FINISHED BLOCK SIZE	FABRIC A	FABRIC B	UNFINISHED UNIT WILL BE
2″ × 2″	(1) 2½″ × 2½″	(2) 1¾″ × 1¾″	2½″ × 2½″
3″ × 3″	(1) 3½″ × 3½″	(2) 2½″ × 2½″	3½″ × 3½″
4″ × 4″	(1) 4½″ × 4½″	(2) 3″ × 3″	4½″ × 4½″
4½″ × 4½″	(1) 5″ × 5″	(2) 3¼″ × 3¼″	5″ × 5″
5″ × 5″	(1) 5½″ × 5½″	(2) 3¾″ × 3¾″	5½″ × 5½″
6″ × 6″	(1) 6½″ × 6½″	(2) 4¼″ × 4¼″	6½″ × 6½″

1. On the wrong side of 2 Fabric B squares, draw a diagonal line from corner to corner.

2. With the right sides together, place a Fabric B square on top of a Fabric A square, matching the raw edges at the top left corner and ensuring that the drawn line runs from side edge to side edge. Sew on the drawn line and then trim the corner, ¼″ from the sewn line. Press.

3. Place the remaining Fabric B square on top of the Fabric A square, matching the raw edges at the bottom right corner and ensuring that the drawn line runs from side edge to side edge. Sew on the drawn line and trim the corner, ¼″ from the sewn line. Press.

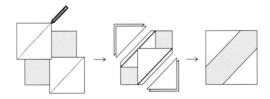

Block 22 | Half-Quarter-Square Triangle *Makes 4 Units*

FINISHED BLOCK SIZE	CUT FABRIC A	CUT FABRIC B	CUT FABRIC C	TRIM SEWN UNIT TO
3″ × 3″	(2) 3⅞″ × 3⅞″	(1) 4¼″ × 4¼″	(1) 4¼″ × 4¼″	3½″ × 3½″
4″ × 4″	(2) 4⅞″ × 4⅞″	(1) 5¼″ × 5¼″	(1) 5¼″ × 5¼″	4½″ × 4½″
4½″ × 4½″	(2) 5⅜″ × 5⅜″	(1) 5¾″ × 5¾″	(1) 5¾″ × 5¾″	5″ × 5″
5″ × 5″	(2) 5⅞″ × 5⅞″	(1) 6¼″ × 6¼″	(1) 6¼″ × 6¼″	5½″ × 5½″
6″ × 6″	(2) 6⅞″ × 6⅞″	(1) 7¼″ × 7¼″	(1) 7¼″ × 7¼″	6½″ × 6½″

1. Using the Fabric B and Fabric C squares, construct two Half-Square Triangles (see page 20). Do not trim the units.

2. On the wrong side of two Fabric A squares, draw a diagonal line from corner to corner.

3. Place a Fabric A square right sides together with a Fabric B/C HST so that the drawn line on Fabric A is perpendicular to the seam line of the Fabric B/C HST.

4. Sew ¼″ to each side of the drawn line.

5. Using a rotary cutter and ruler, cut the block diagonally on the drawn line. Press the units open and trim to size.

6. Repeat Steps 3-5 with the second Fabric A square and Fabric B/C HST.

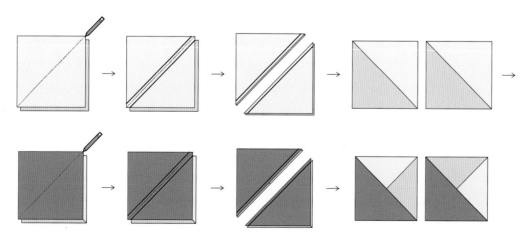

Block 23 | Courthouse Steps   *Makes 1 Unit*

FINISHED BLOCK SIZE	FABRIC FOR SECTION 1	FABRIC FOR SECTIONS 2 & 3	FABRIC FOR SECTIONS 4, 5, 6 & 7	FABRIC FOR SECTIONS 8, 9, 10 & 11	FABRIC FOR SECTIONS 12 & 13	TRIM SEWN UNIT TO
4″ × 4″	1½″ × 1½″	1″ × 1½″	1″ × 2½″	1″ × 3½″	1″ × 4½″	4½″ × 4½″
4½″ × 4½″	1⅝″ × 1⅝″	1⅛″ × 1⅝″	1⅛″ × 2⅞″	1⅛″ × 4⅛″	1⅛″ × 5⅜″	5″ × 5″
5″ × 5″	1¾″ × 1¾″	1⅛″ × 1¾″	1⅛″ × 3″	1⅛″ × 4¼″	1⅛″ × 5½″	5½″ × 5½″
6″ × 6″	2″ × 2″	1¼″ × 2″	1¼″ × 3½″	1¼″ × 5″	1¼″ × 6½″	6½″ × 6½″

1. Using the chart above, cut one fabric for each Section.

2. Copy the Courthouse Steps foundation piecing pattern (see page 139) to the appropriate size for your project.

3. Foundation paper piece (see page 129) the block, leaving a ¼″ seam allowance around the outside edges.

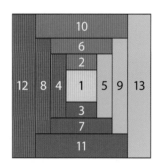

Block 24 | # Diamond-in-a-Rectangle *Makes 1 Unit*

1. Copy the Diamond-in-a-Rectangle foundation piecing pattern (see page 137) to the appropriate size.

2. Cut a Fabric B rectangle in half diagonally from top left to bottom right. Cut the remaining Fabric B rectangle in half diagonally from top right to bottom left.

3. Foundation paper piece the block (see page 129) leaving a ¼″ seam allowance around the outside edges.

FINISHED BLOCK SIZE	FABRIC A	FABRIC B	TRIM SEWN UNIT TO
1½″ × 3″	(1) 2″ × 3½″	(2) 1¾″ × 3¼″	2″ × 3½″
2″ × 4″	(1) 2½″ × 4½″	(2) 2″ × 4″	2½″ × 4½″
2½″ × 5″	(1) 3″ × 5½″	(2) 2½″ × 5″	3″ × 5½″
3″ × 6″	(1) 3½″ × 6½″	(2) 3″ × 6″	3½″ × 6½″

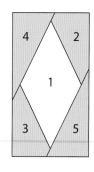

Block 25 | # House   *Makes 1 Unit*

1. Draw a diagonal line from corner to corner on the wrong side of both Fabric B squares.

2. Place a marked square on top of the Fabric A square, right sides together and matching the raw edges at the top left corner. Ensure that the drawn line runs from side edge to side edge. Sew on the drawn line. Trim the corner ¼˝ from the stitching and press.

3. Sew the second Fabric B square on the top right corner of the Fabric A square, using the same process as in Step 2 above, and press.

FINISHED BLOCK SIZE	FABRIC A	FABRIC B	TRIM SEWN UNIT TO
2˝ × 2˝	(1) 2½˝ × 2½˝	(2) 1½˝ × 1½˝	2½˝ × 2½˝
3˝ × 3˝	(1) 3½˝ × 3½˝	(2) 2˝ × 2˝	3½˝ × 3½˝
4˝ × 4˝	(1) 4½˝ × 4½˝	(2) 2½˝ × 2½˝	4½˝ × 4½˝
4½˝ × 4½˝	(1) 5˝ × 5˝	(2) 2¾˝ × 2¾˝	5˝ × 5˝
5˝ × 5˝	(1) 5½˝ × 5½˝	(2) 3˝ × 3˝	5½˝ × 5½˝
6˝ × 6˝	(1) 6½˝ × 6½˝	(2) 3½˝ × 3½˝	6½˝ × 6½˝

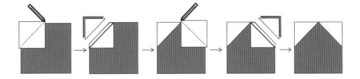

Block 26 | # O Block *Makes 1 Unit*

1. Determine which style of appliqué you will use (see page 128) and add a seam allowance if necessary. Cut the O Template (see pages 135-136) from the Fabric B square.

2. Crease the Fabric A square in half lengthwise. Open the Fabric A square and fold it widthwise and make a second crease. Fold the "O" in the same manner.

3. Using the creases as guides, center the "O" on top of the Fabric A square and appliqué the "O" into place.

FINISHED BLOCK SIZE	FABRIC A (BACKGROUND)	FABRIC B	UNFINISHED UNIT WILL BE
3″ × 3″	(1) 3½″ × 3½″	(1) 3″ × 3″	3½″ × 3½″
4″ × 4″	(1) 4½″ × 4½″	(1) 4″ × 4″	4½″ × 4½″
4½″ × 4½″	(1) 5″ × 5″	(1) 4½″ × 4½″	5″ × 5″
5″ × 5″	(1) 5½″ × 5½″	(1) 5″ × 5″	5½″ × 5½″
6″ × 6″	(1) 6½″ × 6½″	(1) 6″ × 6″	6½″ × 6½″

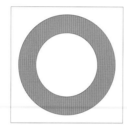

Block 27 | # Pinwheel   *Makes 1 Unit*

1. Make 4 Half-Square Triangles (see page 20) with the Fabric A and Fabric B squares. If necessary, trim to the size indicated in the adjacent chart.

2. Arrange the blocks into a 4-patch. Sew the blocks into rows and the rows into a completed pinwheel.

FINISHED BLOCK SIZE	FABRICS A & B	TRIM HST TO	UNFINISHED UNIT WILL BE
4″ × 4″	(2) 3″ × 3″	(4) 2½″ × 2½″	4½″ × 4½″
4½″ × 4½″	(2) 3¼″ × 3¼″	(4) 2¾″ × 2¾″	5″ × 5″
5″ × 5″	(2) 3½″ × 3½″	(4) 3″ × 3″	5½″ × 5½″
6″ × 6″	(2) 4″ × 4″	(4) 3½″ × 3½″	6½″ × 6½″

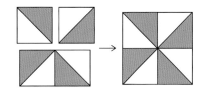

Block 28 | # Snowball   *Makes 1 Unit*

1. Draw a diagonal line from corner to corner on the wrong side of all Fabric B squares.

2. With the right sides together and matching the raw edges, place one Fabric B square at the top left corner of the Fabric A square and ensure that the drawn line runs from side edge to side edge. Sew on the drawn line and then trim the corner ¼" from the sewn line. Press.

3. Using the remaining Fabric B squares, repeat Step 2 for the 3 corners of the Fabric A square.

FINISHED BLOCK SIZE	FABRIC A	FABRIC B	TRIM SEWN UNIT TO
3″ × 3″	(1) 3½″ × 3½″	(4) 1½″ × 1½″	3½″ × 3½″
4″ × 4″	(1) 4½″ × 4½″	(4) 1¾″ × 1¾″	4½″ × 4½″
4½″ × 4½″	(1) 5″ × 5″	(4) 2″ × 2″	5″ × 5″
5″ × 5″	(1) 5½″ × 5½″	(4) 2¼″ × 2¼″	5½″ × 5½″
6″ × 6″	(1) 6½″ × 6½″	(4) 2½″ × 2½″	6½″ × 6½″

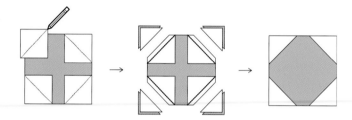

Block 29 | Friendship Star *Makes 1 Unit*

1. Make 4 HSTs (see page 20) with the larger Fabric A and Fabric B squares.

2. Arrange the HSTs with the smaller Fabric A and Fabric B squares into a 9-patch.

3. Sew into 3 rows of 3 blocks each and then sew the 3 rows together.

FINISHED BLOCK SIZE	FABRIC A	FABRIC B	TRIM HST TO	UNFINISHED UNIT WILL BE
3″ × 3″				3½″ × 3½″
	(1) 1½″ × 1½″ (2) 2″ × 2″	(4) 1½″ × 1½″ (2) 2″ × 2″	(4) 1½″ × 1½″	
4½″ × 4½″				5″ × 5″
	(1) 2″ × 2″ (2) 2½″ × 2½″	(4) 2″ × 2″ (2) 2½″ × 2½″	(4) 2″ × 2″	
6″ × 6″				6½″ × 6½″
	(1) 2½″ × 2½″ (2) 3″ × 3″	(4) 2½″ × 2½″ (2) 3″ × 3″	(4) 2½″ × 2½″	

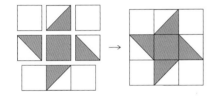

Block 30 | Spool *Makes 1 Unit*

FINISHED BLOCK SIZE	FABRIC A	FABRIC B	FABRIC C	TRIM SEWN UNIT TO
4″ × 4″				4½″ × 4½″
	(1) 2½″ × 2½″	(2) 1½″ × 4½″	(2) 1½″ × 2½″	
			(4) 1½″ × 1½″	
5″ × 5″				5½″ × 5½″
	(1) 3″ × 3″	(2) 1¾″ × 5½″	(2) 1¾″ × 3″	
			(4) 1¾″ × 1¾″	
6″ × 6″				6½″ × 6½″
	(1) 3½″ × 3½″	(2) 2″ × 6½″	(2) 2″ × 3½″	
			(4) 2″ × 2″	

1. Draw a diagonal line from corner to corner on the wrong side of all the Fabric C squares.

2. With the right sides together and matching the raw edges, place a Fabric C square on a Fabric B rectangle. Sew on the drawn line and then trim the corner ¼″ from the sewn line. Press.

3. Sew a Fabric C square on the opposite end of the Fabric B rectangle in the same manner, noting the orientation of the stitching in the illustration below.

4. Repeat Steps 2 and 3 for the remaining 2 Fabric C squares and Fabric B rectangle.

5. Sew a Fabric C rectangle to the left and right edges of the Fabric A square. Press.

6. Arrange the 3 rows and sew the rows together to form the block. Press.

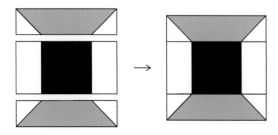

Chapter 3

The Medallions

Medallion 1 | # Peels and Paths *Finished Size: 24″ square*

This medallion has an overall diamond shape, which is softened by using two different curved shapes. The drunkard's path blocks have more background space than the ones I typically use, which helps keep the scale of the curves smaller. I love hand sewing so I chose to hand-appliqué the peels, but they will look just as good if you choose to sew them by machine.

MATERIALS

Fabric A: ⅝ yard Blue for the background

Fabric B: 1 fat quarter Yellow print

Fabric C: 9″ square White print

Fabric D: 9″ square Coral print

Fabric E: 12″ square Green print

Modified Drunkard's Path Templates A and B (see page 137)

4″ Peel Template (see page 134)

Circle Template, (see page 135)

CUTTING

From Fabric A, cut:
(4) 4½″ × WOF strips
    sub-cut into:
        (24) 4½″ squares
        12 Modified Drunkard's Path Quarter Arches using Template B

From Fabric B, cut:
8 Modified Drunkard's Path Quarter Circles using Template A
(1) 3″ square for the center Circle

From Fabric C, cut:
4 Modified Drunkard's Path Quarter Circles using Template A

From Fabric D, cut:
(4) 4″ Peel shapes
    *Note: For seam allowance instructions, refer to page 46

From Fabric E, cut:
(8) 4″ Peel shapes
    *Note: For seam allowance instructions, refer to page 46

Assembly

1. Construct 8 Fabric A/B and 4 Fabric A/C Modified Drunkard's Path blocks using the Drunkard's Path (see page 32) instructions.

2. Using your preferred method, appliqué (see page 128) 4 Fabric D and 8 Fabric E 4″ Peels (see page 46) to the remaining Fabric A squares.

3. Position the units into (9) 4-patch units, referring to the Assembly Diagram (adjacent). Arrange the units into a 9-patch to form the medallion, and assemble accordingly. Press the seams in one direction.

4. Appliqué the circle in the center of the assembled block.

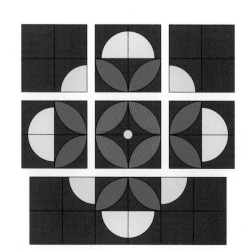

Assembly Diagram

Medallion 2 | # Dogwood *Finished Size: 20˝ square*

I have always loved the double wedding ring quilt, but have never tried my hand at making one. I also like that a-ha! moment when I discover a secondary pattern made by the repetition of many of the same blocks. While shopping at an antique store, I came across a sweet, vintage double wedding ring quilt. It was green and scrappy and so lovely, but what really caught my eye was the four-petal blossom made where four ring sets met. It immediately reminded me of the flower of the dogwood tree, a definite harbinger of spring where I live. And while someday I would love to tackle a bed-sized double wedding ring quilt, this medallion is a great start and a fun focal point for any quilt you choose to create.

MATERIALS

Fabric A: ½ yard Green solid for the background

Fabric B: 6 assorted Orange, Pink and Yellow prints for rings, about one fat quarter in total

Fabric C: (1) 4˝ × 8˝ rectangle Hot Pink for the centers and ends

8 copies of the Ring Foundation Paper pattern (see page 138)

1 copy of the Melon Template (see page 138)

1 copy of the Arc Template (see page 138)

CUTTING

From Fabric A, cut:
(2) 1½˝ × WOF

    sub-cut into:

      (2) 1½˝ × 18½˝ rectangles

      (2) 1½˝ × 20½˝ rectangles

  8 Arcs using the template

  4 Melons using the template

From Fabric B, cut:
(8) 2½˝ × 3˝ pieces from each of 6 prints for 48 total.

From Fabric C, cut:
(8) 2˝ squares

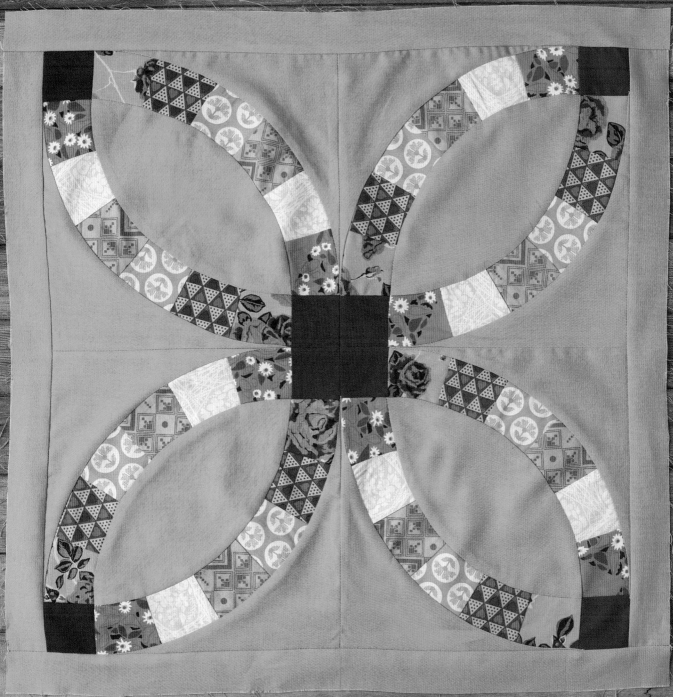

Assembly

1. Enlarge and cut the Ring Foundation Paper patterns along the cut line. Foundation paper piece (see page 129) 8 Rings.

2. With the paper facing up, trim each Ring so the excess fabric is cut away, but keep the paper attached. Divide the Rings into two groups of four Rings each. Remove the foundation papers from one group of Rings and set the remaining group of Rings aside for Step 4. (Fig. 1)

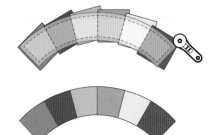

Figure 1

3. Attach the Rings to the Melons. Fold each of the 4 Fabric C Melons in half, matching the end points and making a crease to mark the center. Pin 1 Melon to 1 Ring (with the foundation papers removed) matching the raw edges, ends and centers. Ease the fabric across the curve, pin and sew in place. Press the seams towards the Melon. Repeat for the remaining 3 Melons.

4. Sew a 2″ Fabric C square to each end of the 4 Rings . Press the seams towards the Fabric C squares. Remove the foundation papers from the 4 Rings. Pin these Rings to the opposite edge of each Melon as in Step 3. Make sure to match the seams, raw edges, ends and centers. Sew and then press the seams towards the Melon.

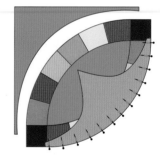

Figure 2

5. Attach the Arcs. Fold one Arc in half, matching the ends, and making a crease to mark the center. Pin the Arc to the Ring, matching the centers. Pin each end of the Arc to the Ring so that the raw edge extends ¼″ past the seam of the Fabric C square and its neighboring Ring end (Fig 2). Ease the fabric across the curve, pin and sew in place. Press the seam towards the Arc. Repeat in the same manner with a second Arc on the opposite side of the Ring (Fig. 3). Repeat Step 5 with the remaining 3 Ring sets and 6 Arcs.

6. Referencing the Assembly Diagram, arrange and sew the blocks into a 4-Patch to create the medallion.

7. Sew a 1½″ × 18½″ Fabric A strip to the left and right sides of the medallion. Press the seams towards the Fabric A strips. Then, attach a 1½″ × 20½″ Fabric A strip to the top and bottom edges of the medallion. Press the seams towards the Fabric A strips.

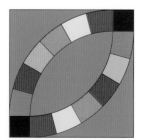

Figure 3

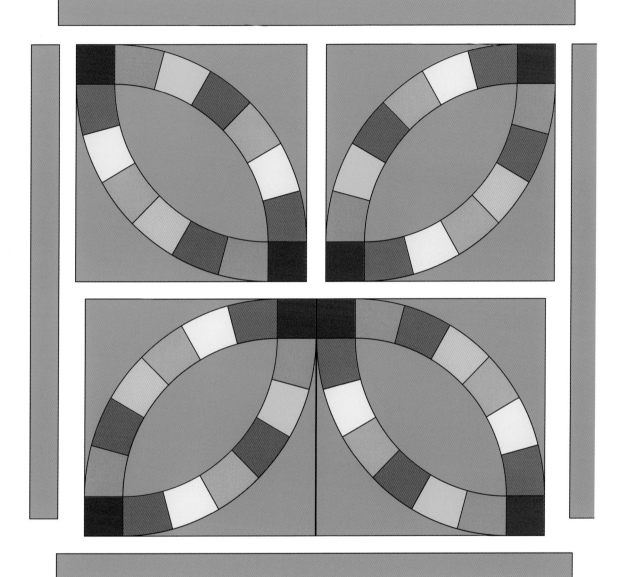

Assembly Diagram

Medallion 3 | # Box Canyon *Finished Size: 30˝ square*

Starting a medallion quilt with an over-sized block is a wonderful way to make a big statement in a little time, too! This medallion certainly fits that bill with its large center star and corner units. The variety of shapes—diamonds, squares and triangles—offers great design opportunities for whatever blocks and borders you choose to add.

MATERIALS

Fabric A: 1 yard low volume print for background

Fabric B: 1 fat quarter Green print for star points

Fabric C: 1 fat quarter Brown print for centers and borders

Fabric D: ⅝ yard Pink solid for corner units

CUTTING

From Fabric A, cut:
(2) 5½˝ × WOF strips
  sub-cut into:
   (4) 5½˝ × 10½˝ rectangles
   (4) 5½˝ squares
(3) 3˝ × WOF strips
  sub-cut into:
   (32) 3˝ squares
(4) 3½˝ squares
(2) 6˝ squares

From Fabric B, cut:
(8) 5½˝ squares

From Fabric C, cut:
(1) 10½˝ square
(4) 5½˝ squares

From Fabric D, cut:
(2) 5½˝ × WOF strips
  sub-cut into:
   (24) 5½˝ × 3˝ rectangles
(2) 6˝ squares
(4) 3½˝ squares
(4) 3˝ squares

Assembly

1. Construct a 10″ Square-in-a-Square block (see page 37) using the 10½″ Fabric C square and (4) 5½″ Fabric A squares. The unit will be 10½″ square.

2. Construct (4) 5″ × 10″ Flying Geese blocks (see page 21) using the (4) 5½″ × 10½″ Fabric A rectangles and the (8) 5½″ Fabric B squares. The units will be 5½″ × 10½″.

3. Construct (4) 5″ Half-Square Triangles (see page 20) using the (2) 6″ Fabric A squares and the (2) 6″ Fabric D squares. Trim to 5½″ square.

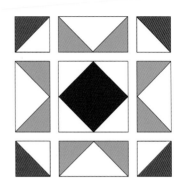

Figure 1

4. Arrange the assembled units for the Center of the medallion (Fig. 1). Sew the units into 3 rows and the 3 rows together to form the center star.

5. Construct (8) 2½″ × 5″ Flying Geese units using the (8) 5½″ × 3″ Fabric D rectangles and (16) 3″ Fabric A squares. The units will be 3″ × 5½″.

6. Construct (8) 2½″ × 5″ left-leaning Chisels and (8) 2½″ × 5″ right-leaning Chisels (see page 42) using the (16) 3″ × 5½″ Fabric D rectangles and (16) 3″ Fabric A squares. The units will be 3″ × 5½″.

7. Referencing the Assembly Diagram (opposite), arrange and sew a Border unit using 2 left-leaning and 2 right-leaning Chisel blocks, 2 Flying Geese Blocks and a Fabric C square. Repeat to create a total of 4 Border units.

8. Sew an assembled Border unit to the left and right sides of the Center. Press the seams towards the outside.

9. Construct (8) 3″ HSTs using the (4) 3½″ Fabric A squares and the (4) 3½″ Fabric D squares. Trim to 3″ square. Arrange the HSTs and remaining Fabric A and D squares into (4) 4-patch units and sew together to form 4 Corner units.

10. Attach an assembled Corner unit from Step 9 to the opposite ends of the 2 remaining Borders from Step 7. Sew the assembled Borders top and bottom of the assembled unit from Step 8. Press the seams towards the outside.

Assembly Diagram

Medallion 4 | # God's Eye *Finished Size: 15″ square*

Have you ever made a god's eye from two sticks and some yarn? Inspired by that classic camp craft, this medallion showcases the interplay between concentric squares of color. I used foundation paper piecing to get those nice mitered corners without any y-seams. If using all solids doesn't appeal to you, try making this with a print or two mixed in for a softer feel.

MATERIALS

A fat eighth of each of these fabrics is more than enough.

Fabric A: Aqua solid

Fabric B: Brown solid

Fabric C: White solid

Fabric D: Orange solid

Fabric E: Dark Green solid

Fabric F: Light Pink solid

Fabric G: Light Green solid

Fabric H: Navy Blue solid

Fabric I: Red solid

4 copies of the Inner Triangle Foundation Pattern A (see page 140)

8 copies of the Half-Corner Triangle Foundation Pattern B (see page 140)

CUTTING

From Fabric A, cut:
(1) 5″ square

> sub-cut on both diagonals to yield 4 quarter-square triangles

From Fabric B, cut:
(4) 1½″ × 5½″ rectangles

From Fabric C, cut:
(4) 2½″ × 9″ rectangles

From Fabric D, cut:
(4) 1½″ × 11″ rectangles

From Fabric E, cut:
(4) 1½″ × 12″ rectangles

From Fabric F, cut:
(2) 3″ squares

> sub-cut on both diagonals to yield 8 quarter-square triangles

From Fabric G, cut:
(8) 1¾″ × 4½″ rectangles

From Fabric H, cut:
(8) 1½″ × 6½″ rectangles

From Fabric I, cut:
(8) 2¼″ × 8½″ rectangles

Assembly

1. Referring to the Assembly Diagram (opposite) for fabric placement, use the inner triangle Template A and Fabrics A, B, C, D and E, foundation paper piece (see page 129) 4 Inner Triangles. Set aside.

2. Referring to the Assembly Diagram for fabric placement, use the half-corner triangle Template B and Fabrics F, G, H and I, foundation paper piece 8 Half-Corner Triangles.

3. Sew 2 Half-Corner Triangle units together along a short side to form a completed Corner Triangle. Repeat with the remaining 6 Half-Corner Triangle units from Step 2 to yield 4 completed Corner Triangles total.

4. Sew an assembled Corner Triangle from Step 3 to an Inner Triangle from Step 1 along their diagonal edges.

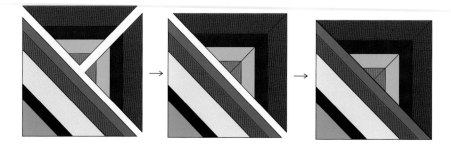

5. Repeat with the remaining assembled Corner triangles from Step 3 and Inner Triangles from Step 1, to create a total of 4 blocks.

6. Arrange and sew the blocks into 4-patch to finish the medallion. Remove the paper from the medallion after it is pieced into the finished quilt to maintain stability.

Assembly Diagram

Medallion 5 | # Lone Star *Finished Size: 18″ square*

Vintage medallion quilts often showcase a large Lone Star block as their medallions. My version is smaller and still a show-stopper! Constructed using strip piecing, it comes together in a snap, too.

MATERIALS

Fabric A: ⅛ yard Navy and White print

Fabric B: ⅛ yard Pink and Red print

Fabric C: ¼ yard Dark Aqua floral

Fabric D: ⅛ yard White and Blue dot

Fabric E: ⅛ yard Red and Gold print

Fabric F: ⅓ yard Aqua solid for background

CUTTING

From Fabrics A and E, cut:
(1) 1¾″ × WOF strip

From Fabrics B and D, cut:
(2) 1¾″ × WOF strips

From Fabric C, cut:
(3) 1¾″ × WOF strips

From Fabric F, cut:
(4) 4⅝″ squares
    sub-cut diagonally
    to yield 8 triangles
(4) 6⅛″ squares
    sub-cut diagonally
    to yield 8 triangles

Assembly

1. To create the pieced diamonds, the strips are sewn into sets and then cut. The beginning edges of each strip should be staggered 1½″ in from the previous strip (Fig. 1). Sew the sets with a ¼″ seam and press the seams open.

Figure 1

The sets are created as follows:

(1) Fabric A ⟶ Fabric B ⟶ Fabric C

(1) Fabric B ⟶ Fabric C ⟶ Fabric D

(1) Fabric C ⟶ Fabric D ⟶ Fabric E

2. Line up the 45° angle on your ruler with the top edge of the strip set and trim the staggered edges sparingly (Fig. 2). Repeat for the remaining 2 strip sets.

3. Measuring in from the trimmed edges, cut (8) 1¾" pieces from each of the 3 strip sets.

4. Arrange 1 piece from each of the 3 strip sets as shown (Fig. 3). Pin the ABC piece to the BCD piece, matching the seams. Sew the pieces together and press the seams open. Pin the CDE piece to the BCD edge of the diamond and sew them together in the same manner.

tip | A little extra care when sewing your strip sets together will ensure that your seam lines match up. It can help to measure and mark the seam allowance at the beginning and end of the sewing line to see that the tips intersect right at the ¼" mark. To double-check that everything is aligned properly before sewing, put a pin through the seam at the sewing line. If the pin comes out through the seam line on the other side, you are good to sew. If it doesn't, shift the pieces until those seams match exactly.

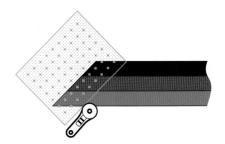

Figure 2

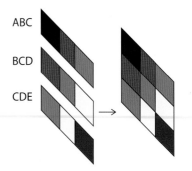

ABC

BCD

CDE

Figure 3

5. Arrange 2 diamonds and 4 rectangles for a Quarter-Star unit as shown in Figure 4 (below), taking care that the Fabric F Half-Square Triangles are placed correctly. Sew the Fabric F triangles in place and press the seams open.

6. Matching the seams and raw edges, sew the Fabric F/Diamond units together along their diagonal edges. Press the seams open.

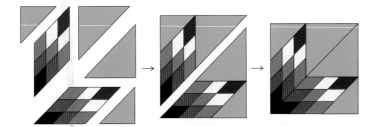

Figure 4

7. Repeat Steps 5-6 for the remaining 3 Quarter-Star units.

8. Referencing the Assembly Diagram (opposite), arrange and sew the Quarter-Star units into a 4-patch, to finish the medallion.

Assembly Diagram

This medallion has movement. The contrast triangles on either side of the medallion star's points make it look like it would spin right off the fabric! If you would like a scrappier look, use different prints for each of the star points to play up the star's diamond shapes.

MATERIALS

1 fat quarter of each of the following

Fabric A: Blue print for the star

Fabric B: Green solid for the setting triangles

Fabric C: White solid for the setting triangles

Fabric D: Yellow solid for the corners

1 copy of the Diamond template (see page 139)

1 copy of the Triangle template (see page 139)

CUTTING

Fabric A: 8 diamonds using the diamond template

Fabric B: 8 triangles using the triangles template

Fabric C: 8 triangles using the triangle template

Fabric D: (2) 4⅜″ squares
  sub-cut diagonally to yield
  4 triangles

Assembly

1. Sew 1 Fabric B triangle to the top left edge of each Fabric A diamond. Sew 1 Fabric C triangle to the top right edge of each Fabric A diamond. Press the seams away from Fabric A. Repeat to create a total of 8 Pieced Triangles.

2. Sew 1 Fabric D triangle to the top edge of 4 Pieced Triangle units to form 4 Corner units. Press the seams towards Fabric D.

3. Sew 1 Pieced Triangle unit from Step 1 to the right edge of each Corner unit (Fig. 1). Press the seams towards the Pieced Triangle units.

4. Referencing the Assembly Diagram (below), arrange and sew two assembled units from Step 3 together and press. Repeat.

5. Carefully matching the seams, sew the 2 assembled units from Step 4 together along the angled edges, press and trim to 12″.

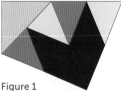

Figure 1

Assembly Diagram

Chapter 4

The Quilts

| *make your own* MEDALLION

make your own MEDALLION

Centerpiece

Finished Quilt Size: 84½″ square

Quilted by Angela Walters

Most of the quilts I make are a combination of solid fabrics and prints. When I drew the design for this quilt, though, there was no doubt in my mind that it would break the mold. All the angled lines and repeating triangles screamed to be cut from solids. Plus, I love the idea of making the traditional medallion quilt more modern by using graphic shapes and loads of negative space.

This is a big quilt, but don't let that deter you. The majority of the piecing happens in a few borders which makes the quilt top come together quicker than you might think. Put on some music or queue up a podcast and chain-piece the day away!

MATERIALS

Fabric A: 1²/₃ yards White

Fabric B: 1¼ yards Navy Blue

Fabric C: 4 yards Gray

Fabric D: ½ yard Pink

Fabric E: ⅝ yard Dark Green

Fabric F: ½ yard Bright Green

Fabric G: ⅜ yard Medium Blue

Fabric H: 1⅛ yard Aqua

Backing Fabric: 7¾ yards

Binding Fabric: ¾ yard

Batting: 2½ yards, 90″ wide

" I love the idea of making the traditional medallion quilt more modern by using graphic shapes and loads of negative space."

CUTTING

Center Medallion

From Fabric A, cut:
- (20) 4″ squares
- (4) 3½″ × 6½″ rectangles

From Fabric B, cut:
- (20) 4″ squares
- (10) 3⅞″ squares
  - sub-cut in half diagonally

From Fabric C, cut:
- (2) 15⅞″ squares
  - sub-cut in half diagonally

From Fabrics D, E, G and H, cut:
- (4) 3½″ × 6½″ rectangles
- (8) 3½″ squares

From Fabric F, cut:
- (2) 3½″ × 6½″ rectangles
- (12) 3½″ squares

Border 1

From Fabric A, cut:
- (16) 3½″ squares

From Fabric C, cut:
- (6) 6½″ × WOF strips
  - sub-cut into:
    - (4) 6½″ × 15½″ strips
    - (4) 6½″ × 21½″ strips

From Fabric F, cut:
- (4) 6½″ squares

Border 2

From Fabric A, cut:
- (16) 3½″ squares
- (56) 4″ squares
- (4) 3½″ × 6½″ rectangles

From Fabric B, cut:
- (64) 4″ squares

From Fabric D, cut:
- (8) 3½″ squares

From Fabric E, cut:
- (8) 3½″ squares
- (2) 3½″ × 6½″ rectangles

From Fabric F, cut:
- (8) 4″ squares

From Fabric G, cut:
- (4) 3½″ squares
- (2) 3½″ × 6½″ rectangles

From Fabric H, cut:
- (8) 3½″ squares
- (4) 3½″ × 6½″ rectangles
- (8) 3½″ × 21½″ strips

Border 3

From Fabric C, cut:
- (8) 3½″ squares
- (4) 3½″ × 30½″ strips
- (4) 3½″ × 33½″ strips

From Fabrics D and E, cut:
- (2) 3½″ × 6½″ rectangles

Border 4

From Fabric C, cut:
- (4) 6½″ × 36½″ strips
- (4) 6½″ × 42½″ strips

Assembly

CENTER MEDALLION: 36˝ square

1. Using the 4˝ Fabric A and Fabric B squares, sew (40) 3˝ finished Half-Square Triangle units (see page 20).

2. Arrange 10 Fabric A/B HST units with the 5 Fabric B half-triangles (Fig. 1). Sew the triangles and squares into rows, pressing the seams in opposite directions so they nest. Join the rows, pressing all the seams in the same direction to yield 1 patchwork triangle. Repeat to create a total of 4 units.

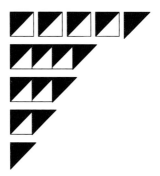

Figure 1: Make 4 units

3. Sew 1 Fabric C triangle to 1 Patchwork Triangle from Step 2 to form a 15½˝ square Large HST unit (Fig 2). Repeat to create a total of 4 Large HST units.

Figure 2: Make 4 units

4. Using Figure 3 for color reference, sew the (22) 3˝ × 6˝ finished Flying Geese units (see page 21) using the 3½˝ × 6½˝ rectangles and 3½˝ squares required for the Center Medallion.

5. Create the center square by joining a B/F Flying Geese pair as shown and press the seams open. (Fig. 3)

Figure 3: Make 1 unit

6. Assemble 4 columns of 5 units each using the remaining Flying Geese, paying close attention to the fabric placement. Press the seams toward the points of the Flying Geese.

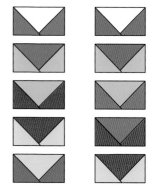

Figure 4: Make 2 columns each unit

7. Attach a Flying Geese column from Step 6 to the left and right of the center square to form the center row of the medallion. Press the seams towards the Flying Geese columns.

8. Sew an assembled Patchwork Half-Square Triangle unit to the left and right of a Flying Geese column from Step 6 to form the top row of the medallion. Press the seams towards the Flying Geese. Repeat to form the bottom row of the medallion.

9. Sew the top and middle rows together, matching the seams. Join the bottom row to the other two rows in the same manner. Press the seams towards the center.

Medallion Assembly Diagram

BORDER ONE: 6˝ wide, swap in any 6˝ finished block for the Square-in-a-Square blocks

1. Using the Fabric A and Fabric F squares, sew (4) 6˝ finished Square-in-a-Square units (see page 37).

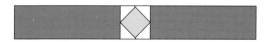

Figure 5

2. Sew a 6½˝ × 15½˝ Fabric C strip to the left and right edges of 2 of the Square-in-a-Square units (Fig. 5). Press the seams towards Fabric C. Attach the borders to the left and right sides of the center medallion. Press the seams towards Border 1.

3. Repeat Step 2 with the remaining Fabric C strips and Square-in-a-Square units, attaching the assembled borders to the top and bottom of the center medallion. Press the seams towards Border 1.

BORDER TWO: 9″ wide

1. Using (56) 4″ Fabric A squares and (56) 4″ Fabric B squares, sew (112) 3″ finished Half-Square Triangle units (see page 20).

2. Divide the 112 HST units into two groups of 56. With Group 1 of 56, and referring to Figure 6, sew 8 rows of 7 HST units each, ensuring that all of the angles point in the same direction. Repeat with the second group of 56 HST units, making sure that the angles in Group 2 point in the OPPOSITE direction than they did in Group 1. (Fig. 6)

Figure 6: Make 8 rows of each group

3. Referencing Figure 7, sew each Group 1 HST row to a 3½″ × 21½″ Fabric H strip. Add a Group 2 HST to the opposite edge of Fabric H. Press the seams towards Fabric H. Repeat to create a total of 8 Sawtooth Border units.

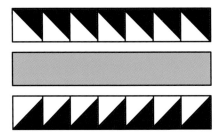

Figure 7: Make 8 units

4. Using the Quilt Assembly Diagram (see page 93) for color reference, sew the (12) 3″ × 6″ finished Flying Geese units required for this Border. Sew the Flying Geese units into 4 sets of 3 units each. Press the seams away from the center Flying Geese unit.

5. Sew a Sawtooth Border block to the left and right Flying Geese units from Step 4 (Fig. 8). Press the seams towards the Flying Geese.

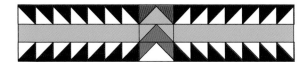

Figure 8: Make 4 units

6. Join an assembled unit from Step 5 to the left and right borders of the quilt, matching the seams and ensuring that the Flying Geese are pointing to the outside edge of the border. Unless otherwise noted, press the seams toward the newly attached border throughout.

7. Using the remaining Fabric B and Fabric F squares, sew (16) 3″ finished HST units. With the remaining Fabric A and Fabric D squares, sew (4) 9″ finished Cog units (see page 38).

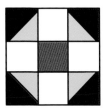

Figure 9: Make 4 units

8. Sew a 9″ finished Cog unit from Step 7 to each end of the top and bottom borders. Press the seams towards the Cog units. Join the top and bottom borders to the quilt, matching the seams and ensuring the Flying Geese are pointing to the outside edge of the border.

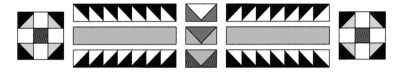

BORDER THREE: 3″ wide

1. Using Fabrics C and E required for Border 3, assemble the (4) 3″ × 6″ finished Flying Geese units (see page 21).

2. Sew a 3½″ × 30½″ Fabric C strip to the left and right of the Flying Geese units. Repeat to create a second border. Referencing the Quilt Assembly Diagram opposite, attach the borders to the left and right sides of the quilt, matching the seams and ensuring that the Flying Geese units are pointing to the outside edge.

3. Repeat Step 2 with the (2) 3½″ × 33½″ Fabric C strips and remaining Flying Geese units, attaching the borders to the top and bottom edges of the quilt.

BORDER FOUR: 6″ wide

1. Sew the (4) 6½″ × 36½″ Fabric C strips into two pairs. Press. Sew the borders to the left and right edges of the quilt, matching the center seams with the Border 3 Flying Geese points.

2. Repeat Step 1 with the (4) 6½″ × 42½″ Fabric C strips, sewing the borders to the top and bottom edges of the quilt.

Finishing

1. Piece the backing to be at least 92″ square.

2. Sandwich, baste and quilt as desired.

3. Square up the quilt and attach the 2½″ wide binding using your preferred method.

Quilt Assembly Diagram

| *make your own* MEDALLION

Studio Window

Finished Quilt Size: 66½˝ square

Quilted by Natalia Bonner

I spend a good part of my days in my sewing room on the third floor of our hundred-plus year old house. The space is a converted attic, with great light, sloped ceilings and walls that are painted an ice blue. There are dormer windows with small bits of yellow and green stained glass and when I look up from the sewing machine, all I see is the tippy top of our Japanese maple tree and the sky beyond. The colors inside and outside that window inspired the palette for this quilt.

This quilt is a wonderful throw size that isn't overwhelming to construct. The pattern contains some basic patchwork shapes and some that are a tiny bit more complicated, but still easily done. There are enough single-fabric borders to break up the piecing, but enough piecing to keep the process interesting. It's a fun one to make!

MATERIALS

Fabric A: 1¼ yards total of various low volume prints

Fabric B: 1 yard total of various Yellow prints

Fabric C: ¾ yard total of various Yellow-Green prints

Fabric D: ⅞ yard total of various Black prints

Fabric E: ⅜ yard total of various light Blue prints

Fabric F: ¼ yard Yellow print for Border 1

Fabric G: ½ yard Light Blue print for Border 3

Fabric H: ⅝ yard Green print for Border 5

Fabric I: 1⅝ yards Light Blue print for Border 7

Backing Fabric: 4¼ yards

Binding Fabric: ⅝ yard

Batting: 2¼ yards, 90˝ wide

4 printed copies each of Patterns A and B (see page 131)

> " *The pattern contains some basic patchwork shapes and some that are a tiny bit more complicated, but still easily done.*"

CUTTING

Center Medallion

From Fabric A, cut:
  (8) 3½˝ × 7˝ rectangles
  (4) 3˝ squares

From Fabric B, cut:
  (4) 3˝ squares

From Fabrics C and E, cut:
  (4) 3˝ × 7˝ rectangles

From Fabric D, cut:
  (8) 3˝ × 5˝ rectangles

Border 1

From Fabrics E and D, cut:
  (2) 3˝ squares

From Fabric F, cut:
  (4) 2½˝ × 12½˝ strips

Border 2

From Fabric A, cut:
  (64) 2½˝ squares

From Fabric C, cut:
  (8) 2½˝ squares
  (32) 2½˝ × 4½˝ rectangles

From Fabric D, cut:
  (8) 2½˝ squares

Border 3

From Fabric B, cut:
  (4) 1½˝ squares

From Fabric C, cut:
  (8) 1½˝ squares
  (8) 1½˝ × 3½˝ rectangles

From Fabric G, cut:
  (4) 3½˝ × 24½˝ strips

Border 4

From Fabrics A and D, cut:
  (24) 3½˝ × 7˝ rectangles

From Fabric B, cut:
  (4) 5½˝ squares

Border 5

From Fabrics D and E, cut:
  (8) 2½˝ squares

From Fabric H, cut:
  (4) 4½˝ × 40½˝ strips

Border 6

From Fabrics A and B, cut:
  (32) 4˝ squares

From Fabric C, cut:
  (4) 3½˝ squares

Border 7

From Fabric B, cut:
  (4) 2½˝ squares

From Fabric D, cut:
  (8) 2½˝ squares
  (8) 2½˝ × 6½˝ rectangles

From Fabric I, cut:
  (4) 6½˝ × 54½˝ strips

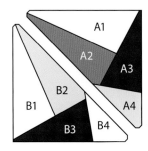

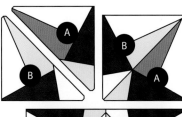

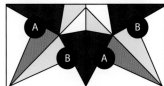

Medallion Assembly Diagram

Assembly

CENTER MEDALLION: 12″ square

1. Photocopy and foundation piece (see page 129) 4 Pattern A and 4 Pattern B units. Refer to the Medallion Assembly Diagram (opposite) for color placement.

2. Sew together the assembled A and B units. Press the seam open. Repeat to create 4 blocks.

3. Arrange and sew into a 4-patch to create the Center Medallion.

BORDER ONE: 2″ wide

1. Attach a Fabric F strip to the left and right edges of the Center Medallion. Unless otherwise noted, press the seams towards the newly attached border throughout.

2. Using the Fabric E and Fabric D squares, sew (4) 2″ finished Half-Square Triangle units.

3. Attach an HST unit (see page 20) to each end of the remaining 2 Fabric F strips, noting the orientation of the HSTs (see the Quilt Assembly Diagram, page 99). Join these to the top and bottom of the Center Medallion.

BORDER TWO: 4″ wide, swap in any 4″ finished block for the 4-Patch blocks

1. Using the Fabric C rectangles and Fabric A squares, sew (32) 2″ × 4″ finished Flying Geese units (see page 21). Join 8 Flying Geese units together for each of the 4 Borders. Press the seams in one direction.

2. Attach a Flying Geese Border to the left and right edges of Border 1.

3. Using the Fabric C and Fabric D squares, sew (4) 4″ finished 4-Patch units (see page 26).

4. Attach (1) 4-Patch unit to each end of the remaining 2 Flying Geese Borders. Join these to the top and bottom of Border 1.

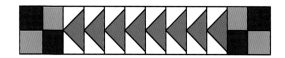

BORDER THREE: 3″ wide, swap in any 3″ finished block for the Dot blocks

1. Attach a Fabric G strip to the left and right edges of Border 2.

2. Using the Fabric B squares and Fabric C squares and rectangles, sew (4) 3″ finished Dot units (see page 36).

3. Referencing the Quilt Assembly Diagram (see page 99), attach a Dot unit to each end of the remaining Fabric G strips. Join these to the top and bottom of Border 2.

BORDER FOUR: 3″ wide

1. Using 12 Fabric A and Fabric D rectangles, sew 24 Right-Leaning Half-Rectangle Triangle units (see page 24). Trim to 3″ × 5½″.

2. Using 12 Fabric A and Fabric D rectangles, sew 24 Left-Leaning HRT units (see page 24). Trim to 3″ × 5½″.

3. Join a Right-Leaning HRT unit to each Left-Leaning HRT unit, taking care that Fabric A and Fabric D alternate. Press the seams in one direction. Join 6 sets of HRT pairs for each of the 4 Borders. Press the seams in one direction.

4. Attach an HRT Border to the left and right edges of Border 3.

5. Referencing the Quilt Assembly Diagram (opposite), sew a Fabric B square to each end of the remaining 2 HRT Borders. Join these to the top and bottom of Border 3.

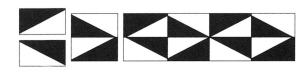

BORDER FIVE: 4″ wide, swap in any 4″ finished block for the 4-Patch blocks

1. Attach a Fabric H strip to the left and right edges of Border 4.

2. Using the Fabric D and Fabric E squares, sew (4) 4″ finished 4-Patch units (see page 26).

3. Referencing the Quilt Assembly Diagram (opposite), attach a 4-Patch unit to each end of the remaining 2 Fabric H strips. Join these to the top and bottom of Border 4.

BORDER SIX: 3″ wide, swap in any 3″ finished block for the HST blocks

1. Using the Fabric A and Fabric B squares, sew (64) 3″ finished HST units (see page 20). Join 16 HST units together for each of the 4 Borders.

2. Attach an HST Border to each of the left and right edges of Border 5.

3. Referencing the Quilt Assembly Diagram (opposite), sew a Fabric C square to each end of the remaining 2 HST borders. Join these to the top and bottom of Border 5.

BORDER SEVEN: 6″ wide, swap in any 6″ finished block for the Dot blocks

1. Attach a Fabric I strip to the left and right edges of Border 6.

2. Using the Fabric B and the Fabric D pieces, sew (4) 6″ finished Dot units (see page 36).

3. Referencing the Quilt Assembly Diagram (opposite), attach a Dot unit to each end of the remaining Fabric I strips. Join these to the top and bottom of Border 6.

Finishing

1. Piece the backing to be at least 74″ × 74″.

2. Sandwich, baste and quilt as desired.

3. Square up the quilt and attach the 2½″ wide binding using your preferred method.

Quilt Assembly Diagram

| *make your own* MEDALLION

Summer Skies

Finished Quilt Size: 72½″ square

Quilted by Natalia Bonner

We are lucky to live on the western edge of the eastern time zone, giving us summer daylight that lasts until after nine o'clock at night. There is something about that time of day when the sun is setting and the sky turns dark blue that I just love. Throw in some pink and orange clouds and you have the makings of one gorgeous summer evening sky.

The center medallion of this quilt is a great example of how you can use a grouping of single blocks to make a statement. Changing up the fabric placement in the blocks creates a strong secondary pattern and foundation paper piecing gives you crisp lines. The final border is a great opportunity to showcase a favorite print or add a big band of a solid color to frame your quilt.

MATERIALS

Fabric A: 1 yard Blue small floral print

Fabric B: 1⅛ yards Gold print

Fabric C: 3 yards Blue floral print

Fabric D: ⅞ yard Pink print

Fabric E: 1⅛ yards White print

Fabric F: ¾ yard Navy solid

Backing Fabric: 4½ yards

Binding Fabric: ⅝ yard

Batting: 2⅓ yards, 90˝ wide

8 copies Kite 6˝ block pattern (see page 136)

8 copies Kite Variation 6˝ block pattern (see page 134)

16 copies Kite Variation 4˝ block pattern (see page 134)

1 copy 4˝ Drunkard's Path Templates A and B (see pages 130 and 132)

1 copy 4˝ Equal-ish Triangle Templates A and B (see page 133)

❝ *The final border is a great opportunity to showcase a favorite print or add a big band of a solid color to frame your quilt.*˝

CUTTING

tip | Border 5 is sewn from continuous pieces of fabric that need to be cut first from the length of Fabric C. Once these cuts are made, cut the Fabric C pieces for the Center Medallion, Border 1 and Border 2 from the remaining fabric.

Center Medallion

From Fabrics A and C, cut:

(8) 5˝ × 7˝ rectangles

sub-cut (4) diagonally from bottom left to top right

sub-cut (4) diagonally from bottom right to top left

From Fabric B, cut:

(8) 4½˝ × 10˝ rectangles

(8) 5˝ × 3˝ rectangles

From Fabric D, cut:

(8) 4½˝ × 8½˝ rectangles

Border 1

From Fabric A, cut:

(16) 4˝ × 2˝ rectangles

From Fabric B, cut:

(16) 3˝ × 5½˝ rectangles

From Fabric C, cut:

(16) 3½˝ × 6˝ rectangles

sub-cut (8) diagonally from bottom left to top right

sub-cut (8) diagonally from bottom right to top left

(48) 4˝ Drunkard's Path quarter-arch pieces

From Fabric E, cut:

(6) 4½˝ × WOF strips

sub-cut into:

(48) 4˝ Drunkard's Path quarter-circle pieces

Border 2

From Fabric C, cut:

(16) 4˝ Drunkard's Path quarter-arch pieces

From Fabric D, cut:

(4) 4½˝ × WOF strips

sub-cut into:

(4) 4½˝ × 24½˝ rectangles

(4) 4½˝ squares

From Fabric E, cut:

(2) 4½˝ × WOF strips

sub-cut into:

(16) 4˝ Drunkard's Path quarter circles

Border 3

From Fabric B, cut:

(5) 2½˝ × WOF

sub-cut into:

(4) 2½˝ × 40½˝ rectangles

(2) 2½˝ × 12½˝ rectangles

(2) 2½˝ × 8½˝ rectangles

Border 4

From Fabric A, cut:

(4) 4½˝ × WOF strips

sub-cut into:

(52) 4˝ Equal-ish Triangles

From Fabric F, cut:

(5) 4½˝ × WOF strips

sub-cut into:

(48) 4˝ Equal-ish Triangles

(4) 4˝ Equal-ish left half Triangles

(4) 4˝ Equal-ish right half Triangles and

(8) 4½˝ squares

Border 5

From Fabric C, cut:

(2) 6½˝ × 60½˝ strips

(2) 6½˝ × 72½˝ strips

Assembly

CENTER MEDALLION: 24″ square

1. Referring to the diagrams for fabric placement, foundation paper piece (see page 129) 4 of each 6″ finished Kite block (see page 39) for Block A and B in each colorway.

Kite Blocks A and B: Make 4 of each colorway

2. Repeat Step 1 to create 4 of each 6″ finished Kite Variation block (see page 40) for Blocks C and D.

Kite Variation Blocks C and D: Make 4 of each colorway

3. Referring to the Mcdallion Assembly Diagram, sew the assembled Blocks into 4 rows of 4 blocks each. Press the seams open. Sew the rows together to form the Center Medallion.

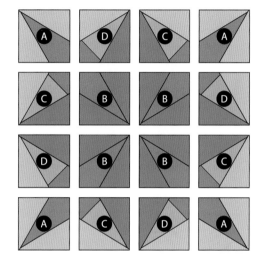

Medallion Assembly Diagram

BORDER ONE: 4″ wide, swap in any 4″ finished block for the Drunkard's Path or Kite Variation blocks

1. Using Fabrics C and E, sew (48) 4″ finished Drunkard's Path blocks (see page 32). Trim to 4½″ square and sew into 4 sets of 12-block Borders.

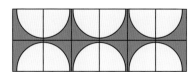

Make 4 Borders

2. Sew a set of Borders to the left and right sides of the Center Medallion. Unless otherwise noted, press the seams towards the newly attached border throughout.

3. Create (16) 4″ finished Kite Variation blocks for Block E. Trim to 4½″ square.

Block E: Make 16

4. Referring to the Quilt Assembly Diagram (see page 105), assemble 4 sets of Block E 4-patches. Attach one to each end of the 2 remaining Borders and sew the top and bottom borders to the Center Medallion.

BORDER TWO: 4˝ wide, swap in any 4˝ finished block for the Drunkard's Path blocks

1. From Fabrics C and E, sew (16) 4˝ Drunkard's Path blocks (see page 32). Trim to 4½˝ square.

2. Referring to the Quilt Assembly Diagram (opposite), sew the Drunkard's Path blocks into 8 sets of 2 blocks each.

3. Sew a set of Drunkard's Path blocks to each end of the (4) 4½˝ × 24½˝ Fabric D rectangles. Press the seams towards Fabric D.

4. Attach a border to the left and right side of Border 1.

5. Sew (1) 4½˝ Fabric D square to each end of the remaining 2 borders. Press the seams towards Fabric D. Join these to the top and bottom of Border 1.

BORDER THREE: 2˝ wide

1. Construct the left and right Borders by sewing each 2½˝ × 8½˝ Fabric B rectangle to a 2½˝ × 40½˝ Fabric B rectangle. Press the seams open and join the borders to the left and right edges of Border 2.

2. Construct the top and bottom Borders by sewing each 2½˝ × 12½˝ Fabric B rectangle to a 2½˝ × 40½˝ Fabric B rectangle. Press the seams open and join the borders to the top and bottom edges of Border 2.

BORDER FOUR: 4˝ wide, swap in any 4˝ finished block for the Equal-ish Triangle blocks

1. Construct (4) 52½˝ long Equal-ish Triangle borders (see page 34) using (1) 4˝ Fabric F left Template B, (13) 4˝ Fabric A Template As, (12) 4˝ Fabric F Template Bs and a 4˝ Fabric F right Template A.

2. Attach a Triangle Border to each of the left and right edges of Border 3 so that the Fabric A triangles are adjacent to Border 3.

3. Sew a 4½˝ Fabric F square to each end of the remaining 2 Triangle Borders. Press the seams towards the square.

4. Attach the remaining Triangle Borders to the top and bottom edges of Border 3 so that the Fabric A triangles are adjacent to Border 3.

BORDER FIVE: 6˝ wide

1. Attach a 6½˝ × 60½˝ Border to each of the left and right sides of Border 4.

2. Attach a 6½˝ × 72½˝ Border to the top and bottom edges of Border 4.

Finishing

1. Piece the backing to be at least 80˝ square.

2. Sandwich, baste and quilt as desired.

3. Square up the quilt and attach the 2½˝ wide binding using your preferred method.

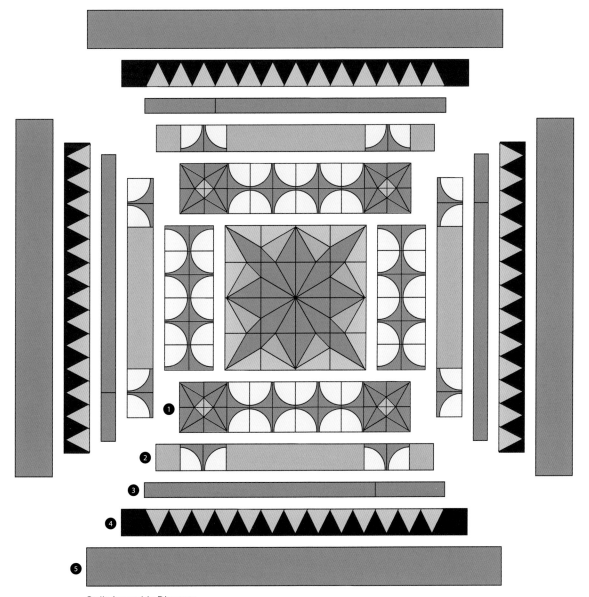

Quilt Assembly Diagram

| *make your own* MEDALLION

Let Love Shine

Finished Quilt Size: 60½˝ square

Quilted by Crinklelove

A good scrap quilt always makes me smile and this one is no exception. The way the colors radiate out from the center heart reminded me of a sun, spreading joy to everything around it. A big dose of bright, happy colors in the borders doesn't hurt, either! Plus, the center medallion of this quilt is just plain fun. Created by piecing rectangles of fabric together and then cutting them into blades, this medallion is a modern rift on the traditional Dresden plate. It's a great opportunity to play with fabric, combining colors and prints in unexpected ways. The small pieces allow you to use scraps or fussy-cut pieces to your heart's content. If scraps aren't your thing, don't worry. This quilt will look amazing in a more curated fabric selection too.

MATERIALS:

Fabric A: 2¾ yards of a low volume print

Fabric B: ½ yard Aqua solid

Fabric C: approximately 2½ yards total of various brightly colored prints (I used navy, aqua, green, yellow, orange and magenta scraps)

Backing Fabric: 4 yards

Binding Fabric: ⅝ yard

Batting: 2 yards, 90″ wide

1 copy of Blade Template (see page 141)

1 copy of the Arch Template (see page 141)

1 copy of the Circle Template (see page 132)

1 copy of the Heart Template (see page 141)

6″ square of cardstock

Aluminum foil

> *The way the colors radiate out from the center heart reminded me of a sun, spreading joy to everything around it.*"

CUTTING

Center Medallion

From Fabric A, cut:
- (20) 3″ × 4″ rectangles
- (1) 4″ square
- (4) Arches using the Template

From Fabric C, cut:
- (20) 4″ × 2½″ rectangles in a variety of colors and prints
- (20) 4″ squares in a variety of colors and prints
- (1) Heart using the Template

Border 1

From Fabric A, cut:
- (2) 3″ squares

From Fabric B, cut:
- (2) 3″ squares
- (4) 2½″ × 20½″ rectangles

Border 2

From Fabric A, cut:
- (3) 2½″ × WOF strips
  sub-cut into:
  - (48) 2½″ squares

From Fabric B, cut:
- (4) 4½″ squares

From Fabric C, cut:
- (48) 2½″ × 4½″ rectangles

Border 3

From Fabric A, cut:
- (2) 2½″ × 32½″ strips
- (2) 2½″ × 36½″ strips

Border 4

From Fabric A, cut:
- (8) 2½″ × WOF strips
  sub-cut into:
  - (84) 2½″ squares
  - (12) 2½″ × 6½″ rectangles
- (1) 6½″ × WOF strip
  sub-cut into:
  - (16) 6½″ × 2½″ rectangles

From Fabric C, cut:

For the Plus blocks, from each of 14 prints, cut:
- (2) 2½″ squares
- (1) 2½″ × 6½″ rectangle

For the Dot blocks, from each of the 14 prints, cut:
- (1) 2½″ square

Border 5

From Fabric A, cut:
- (5) 2½″ × WOF strips
  sub-cut (1) strip into:
  - (2) 2½″ × 8½″ rectangles
  - (2) 2½″ × 12½″ strips
  sub-cut the (4) remaining strips into:
  - (4) 2½″ × 40½″ strips

Border 6

From Fabric A, cut:
- (6) 4½″ × WOF strips
  sub-cut into:
  - (48) 4½″ squares
  - (8) 4½″ × 2½″ rectangles

From Fabric B, cut:
- (4) 4½″ squares

From Fabric C, cut:
- (96) 3″ squares in a variety of colors and prints

Assembly

CENTER MEDALLION: 20˝ square

1. To construct the Blades, sew a Fabric C square to each Fabric C rectangle. Sew a Fabric A rectangle to the Fabric C square to create a total of 20 strip sets. Press the seams away from Fabric A.

2. Divide the strip sets into two groups: 10 sets will have Fabric A on the outside edge of the circle (Group A) and 10 sets will have Fabric C on the outside edge (Group B).

tip | *Before you trim the Blade sets, take the time to arrange them into a circle, alternating Group A and Group B strip sets. Use a design wall to check the balance of the center medallion. This is important because colors and prints relate differently to each other in a circular motif than they do when placed side-by-side. Once you are satisfied with the arrangement, snap a photo. It will come in handy when you assemble the medallion.*

3. Trim the Group A Blade sets to 4˝ × 7½˝ by cutting the excess off the Fabric C rectangles. Trim the Group B Blade sets to 4˝ × 7½˝ by cutting the excess off the Fabric A rectangles.

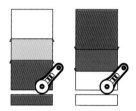

Group A   Group B
Strip Sets: Make 10 Each of Group A and B

4. Cut the Blades as follows: Align the wide end of the Blade Template with the top Fabric A edge of the 10 Group A Blades and trim along the template sides. For the Group B Blades, align the wide edge of the Blade Template with the top Fabric C edge of the Blades and trim along the template sides.

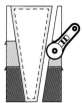 

tip | *Take your time while making the medallion. Its open center can be tricky to manage. You can avoid problems if you lay the blocks on a flat surface and pin them together while flat before sewing them. Sew the seams from the outer edge towards the middle so that the outer curve lines up properly and consider using a spray starch to keep the curved and bias edges from distorting.*

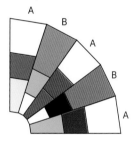 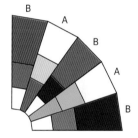

3 Group A Blades: Make 2   3 Group B Blades: Make 2

5. To piece the Quarter Circles, arrange the Blades in 4 sets of 5, alternating Group A and B Blades. 2 Quarter Circle sets should have 3 Group A Blades and the other 2 sets should have 3 Group B Blades. Beginning at the wider, outer edge, with the right sides together, sew the Blades to one another. Press the seams in one direction. Repeat with the remaining sets of Blades to yield 4 Quarter Circles.

6. Fold each Quarter Blade set in half, right sides together matching the long edges. Finger press the fold at the outer edge to mark the center and unfold.

7. Fold each Fabric A Quarter Arch in half right sides together, matching straight edges and ends. Finger press the fold at the inner edge of the arch to mark the center.

8. With the right sides together and matching raw edges, pin the finger pressed center mark of the quarter arch unit to the corresponding center mark of the quarter Blade unit. Next, pin each Quarter Arch side edge to the

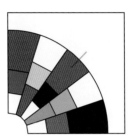 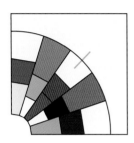

corresponding quarter Blade side edge. Ease the fabric between the center and the sides, pinning in place. Sew together using a ¼˝ seam.

9. Referring to the Medallion Assembly Diagram (below) and with the right sides together, sew the Quarter Circle units into a 4-patch. Take care to ensure that the Group A and Group B Blades alternate. Press all the seams in the same direction.

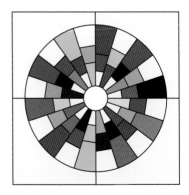

Medallion Assembly Diagram

10. To appliqué the center circle, cut the Circle Template out of card stock. Place it in the center of the 4˝ Fabric A square. Cut around the template adding a scant ½˝ seam allowance.

11. Place the fabric right side down on a 6˝ square of aluminum foil with the card stock template centered on top. Fold the aluminum foil and fabric up over the edges of the template, little by little, smoothing out any wrinkles. Using a hot iron, press the edges all around the circle. Flip the circle over to the other side and repeat. Wait for the foil to cool and then slowly peel it away from the fabric. Remove the card stock template.

12. Lay the Medallion on a flat surface and center the circle over the middle. The circle should cover the raw edges of the hole by about ½˝. Pin or baste the circle in place and then appliqué (see page 128) to the Medallion. Repeat for the Heart appliqué using a 4˝ square of aluminum foil.

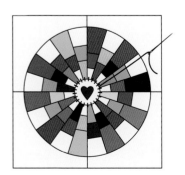

BORDER ONE: 2″ wide, swap in any 2″ finished block for the HST blocks

1. Referring to the Quilt Assembly Diagram (see page 113), sew a 2½″ × 20½″ rectangle to the left and right edges of the Medallion. Press the seams towards Border 1.

2. Using the Fabric A and B squares, assemble (4) 2″ finished Half-Square Triangle units (see page 20).

3. Attach an HST unit to each end of the remaining two Fabric B strips. Sew these to the top and bottom edges of the Medallion. Unless otherwise noted, press the seams toward the newly attached border throughout.

BORDER TWO: 4″ wide, swap in any 2″ × 4″ finished block for the Chisel blocks

1. Using (24) 2½″ × 4½″ Fabric C rectangles and (24) 2½″ Fabric A squares, construct 24 right-leaning 2″ × 4″ finished Chisel blocks (see page 42).

2. Using the remaining (24) 2½″ × 4½″ Fabric C rectangles and (24) 2½″ Fabric A squares, construct 24 left-leaning 2″ × 4″ finished Chisel blocks (see page 42).

3. Sew a left-leaning Chisel to a right-leaning Chisel for a total of 24 pairs of Chisels. Press the seams open.

4. Sew 6 pairs of Chisels together to form one border. Repeat for a total of 4 Chisel Borders.

5. Sew a Chisel Border to the left and right edges of Border 1 so that the Fabric A end of each chisel is adjacent to Border 1.

6. Sew a 4½″ Fabric B square to each end of the remaining 2 Borders and attach to the top and bottom edges of Border 1 so that the Fabric A end of each Chisel is adjacent to Border 1.

BORDER THREE: 2″ wide

1. Sew a 2½″ × 32½″ strip to the left and right edges of Border 2. Press the seams towards Border 3.

2. Sew a 2½″ × 36½″ strip to the top and bottom edges of Border 2. Press the seams towards Border 3.

BORDER FOUR: 6″ wide, swap in any 6″ finished block for the Plus or Dot blocks

1. Using the 14 sets of Fabric C Plus Block squares and rectangles together with (56) 2½″ Fabric A squares, construct (14) 6″ finished Plus units (see page 31).

2. Using the 14 Fabric C Dot block squares, (28) 2½″ Fabric A squares and (28) 2½″ × 6½″ Fabric A rectangles, construct (14) 6″ Dot units (see page 36).

3. To make each side Border, sew 3 Plus units alternating with the 3 Dot units into a row of 6 blocks. Sew a Border with a Dot unit on its top edge to the left edge of Border 3 and sew a Border with a Plus unit at its top edge to the right edge of Border 3.

4. To make the top and bottom Borders, sew 4 Plus units alternating with the 4 Dot units into 2 rows of 8 blocks each. Sew a Border with a Plus unit on its left edge to the top edge of Border 3. Referring to the Quilt Assembly Diagram (opposite), sew a Border with a Dot unit on its left edge to the bottom edge of Border 3.

BORDER FIVE: 2″ wide

1. Sew each 2½″ × 8½″ Fabric A rectangle to a 2½″ × 40½″ Fabric A strip to form the left and right borders. Attach these to the left and right edges of Border 4. Press the seams towards Border 5.

2. Sew each 2½″ × 12½″ Fabric A rectangle to a 2½″ × 40½″ Fabric A strip to form the top and bottom borders. Sew these to the top and bottom edges of Border 4. Press the seams towards Border 5.

BORDER SIX: 4″ wide, swap in any 4″ finished block for the Diagonal Dash blocks

1. Using the (48) 4½″ Fabric A squares and the (96) 3″ Fabric C squares, construct (48) 4″ finished Diagonal Dash units (see page 48).

2. Sew the Diagonal Dash units into 24 pairs, so that the Fabric A angles meet to form a "V". Press the seams open.

3. Sew 6 pairs of Diagonal Dash units together to form one border. Repeat for a total of 4 Dash Borders.

4. Sew a 2½″ × 4½″ Fabric A rectangle to opposite ends of the 4 Diagonal Dash Borders.

5. Referring to the Quilt Assembly Diagram (opposite), sew a Diagonal Dash Border to the left and right edges of Border 5.

6. Sew a 4½″ Fabric B square to each edge of the remaining two borders. Sew a Border to the top and bottom edges of Border 5, matching the orientation of the side borders.

Finishing

1. Piece the backing to be at least 68″ × 68″.

2. Sandwich, baste and quilt as desired.

3. Square up the quilt and attach the 2½″ wide binding using your preferred method.

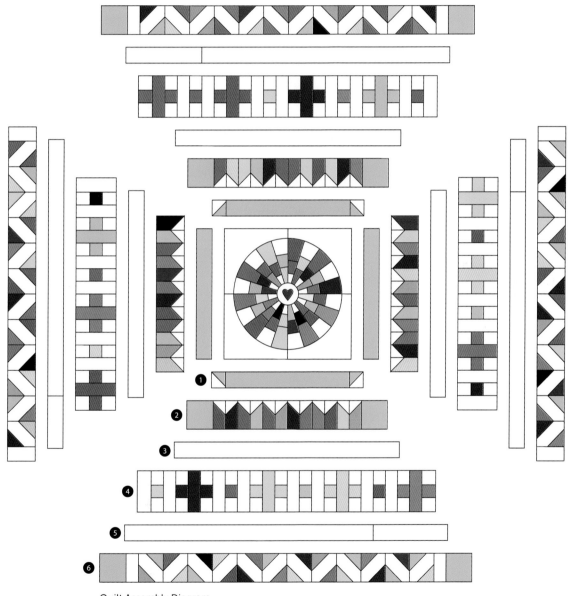

Quilt Assembly Diagram

Tulip Garden

Finished Quilt Size: 60½″ square

Quilted by Crinklelove

I am a doodler and have been drawing little patterns and motifs on bits of paper from the time I could hold a pencil. I love to draw flowers, especially tulips, and have always wanted to make a quilt to reflect my favorite flower motif. Putting a group of them in a medallion was the next logical step! I framed the group of flowers with a variety of angled blocks to create motion and then used some simple pieced borders to quiet it down just a little bit. As I was sketching the design, I loved how the connected X blocks in the final border mimicked a trellis. Perfect for a garden of tulips, if you ask me.

MATERIALS

Fabric A: ½ yard Coral print

Fabric B: ¼ yard Yellow solid

Fabric C: ⅜ yard Mint print

Fabric D: 1½ yards White solid

Fabric E: 1⅛ yards Gray gingham

Fabric F: ½ yard Aqua print

Fabric G: ½ yard Pink print

Fabric H: ½ yard White floral print

Fabric I: ¾ yard Yellow print

Fabric J: ⅜ yard Pink and Coral print

Backing Fabric: 4 yards-pieced to at least 68″ square

Binding Fabric: ⅝ yard

Batting: 2 yards, 90″ wide

" *As I was sketching the design, I loved how the connected X Blocks in the final border mimicked a trellis.*"

CUTTING

Center Medallion

From Fabric A, cut:
- (4) 2½″ squares
- (4) 3″ squares

From Fabric B, cut:
- (4) 1½″ squares

From Fabric C, cut:
- (2) 3″ squares
- (8) 2½″ × 4½″ rectangles

From Fabric D, cut:
- (4) 1½″ squares
- (4) 1½″ × 2½″ rectangles
- (8) 2½″ squares
- (6) 3″ squares

Frorm Fabric E, cut:
- (4) 1½″ × 6½″ rectangles
- (4) 1½″ × 13½″ rectangles

From Fabric F, cut:
- (5) 1½″ squares

From Fabric G, cut:
- (3) 6¼″ squares
  sub-cut diagonally twice

From Fabric H, cut:
- (2) 6¼″ squares
  sub-cut diagonally twice
- (2) 5⅞″ squares
  sub-cut once diagonally

Border 1

From Fabric C, cut:
- (4) 4″ squares
- (4) 4⅜″ squares
  sub-cut once diagonally
  to yield 8 triangles

From Fabrics D and E, cut:
- (2) 2¼″ × WOF strips

From Fabric I, cut:
- (2) 8⅛″ squares
  sub-cut once diagonally to
  yeild 4 triangles

Border 2

From Fabric E, cut:
- (2) 2¼″ × 29″ strips
- (2) 2¼″ × 32½″ strips

Border 3

From Fabric A, cut:
- (16) 4⅞″ squares

From Fabric B, cut:
- (4) 2½″ squares
- (4) 3″ squares

From Fabric C, cut:
- (4) 1½″ squares

From Fabric D, cut:
- (4) 1½″ squares
- (4) 1½″ × 2½″ rectangles
- (4) 3″ squares

From Fabrics G and J, cut:
- (8) 5¼″ squares

Border 4

From Fabric E, cut:
- (8) 2″ × WOF strips

From Fabric G, cut:
- (4) 4½″ squares

From Fabric H, cut:
- (4) 1½″ × WOF strips

Border 5

From Fabric D, cut:
- (6) 6½″ × WOF strips
  sub-cut into:
  (36) 6½″ squares, further
  sub-cut once diagonally
  to yield 72 triangles

From Fabrics F and I, cut:
- (9) 1½″ × WOF strips
  sub-cut into:
  (36) 1½″ × 10″ rectangles

Assembly

CENTER MEDALLION: 20˝ square, swap in any 6˝ finished block for the Tulip blocks

1. Using the 3˝ Fabric A and Fabric D squares, sew (8) 2˝ finished Half-Square Triangles units (see page 20).

2. Sew (4) 6˝ finished Tulip blocks (see page 41) using the HSTs from Step 1, (4) 2½˝ Fabric A squares, (4) 1½˝ Fabric B squares, (4) 1½˝ Fabric D squares and (4) 1½˝ × 2½˝ Fabric D rectangles.

3. Sew (4) left-leaning and (4) right-leaning Chisel units (see page 42), using the 2½˝ Fabric D squares and the 2½˝ × 4½˝ Fabric C rectangles.

4. Sew (4) 2˝ finished HST units using (2) 3˝ Fabric C squares and (2) 3˝ Fabric D squares.

5. Sew a right-leaning Chisel unit to the left edge of each of the Tulip units.

6. Sew a Fabric C/D HST to the bottom edge of each left-leaning Chisel unit. Make sure the HSTs are pointing in the correct direction. Sew 1 unit to the bottom edge of each Tulip unit.

7. Arrange the completed blocks into 2 rows with the flowers pointing towards the outer corners. Sew a 1½˝ × 6½˝ Fabric E rectangle between 2 Tulip units. Repeat with the remaining 2 units Press the seams towards Fabric E.

8. Sew a 1½˝ Fabric F square between the remaining (2) 1½˝ × 6½˝ Fabric E rectangles. Press the seams towards Fabric E. Sew this strip between the 2 rows of Tulip units. Press the seams towards Fabric E.

9. Sew a 1½˝ × 13½˝ Fabric E rectangle to the left and right edges of the assembled unit from Step 8. Press the seams away from the Tulip units.

10. Sew a 1½˝ Fabric F square to each edge of the remaining 1½˝ × 13½˝ Fabric E rectangles and attach to the top and bottom edges of the assembled unit from Step 9. Press the seams away from the Tulip units.

11. Arrange 3 Fabric G and 2 same size Fabric H triangles into a row, alternating prints and matching the shorter sides of the triangles. Sew the triangles together. Press the seams towards fabric G. Repeat to create a total of 4 rows.

12. Sew a triangle row to the left and right sides of the assembled unit from Step 10.

13. Repeat Step 12 to sew the remaining 2 triangle rows to the top and bottom edges. Press the seams towards the Tulip units.

14. Sew a Fabric H corner triangle to each of the 4 corners. Press the seams towards the Tulip units to complete the Center Medallion.

Medallion Assembly Diagram

BORDER ONE: CORNER UNITS

1. Sew a 2¼˝ × WOF Fabric D strip to each 2¼˝ × WOF Fabric E strip. Press the seams towards Fabric E. Sub-cut the strip sets to yield (8) 4˝ × 7¾˝ pieces.

2. Sew a Fabric C triangle to the left edge of 4 strip set pieces (Fig. 1). Press the seams towards the strip set.

3. Sew a strip set/triangle unit to 1 short side of each Fabric I triangle, as shown. Press the seams towards the strip set.

4. Sew a Fabric C triangle to the right edge and a Fabric C square to the left edge of each of the remaining strip set pieces. Press the seams towards the strip set.

5. Sew a triangle unit from Step 3 to an assembled unit from Step 4 (Fig. 2). Repeat to create a total of 4 Corner Units.

6. Referencing the Quilt Assembly Diagram (opposite), attach a Corner Unit to each side of the Medallion. Unless otherwise noted, press the seams towards the newly attached border throughout.

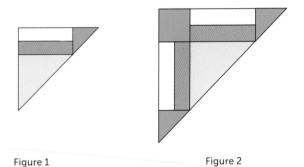

Figure 1   Figure 2

BORDER TWO: 1¾˝ wide

1. Sew a 2¼˝ × 29˝ Fabric E rectangle to the left and right edges of Border 1. Press.

2. Sew a 2¼˝ × 32½˝ Fabric E rectangle to the top and bottom edges of Border 1. Press.

BORDER THREE: 4˝ wide, swap in any 4˝ finished block for the Quarter-HST or Tulip blocks

1. Using the Fabric A, Fabric G and Fabric J squares, sew (32) 4˝ finished Quarter-HST units (see page 22). Trim to 4½˝ square.

2. Using the Fabric B, Fabric C and Fabric D squares and rectangles, sew (4) 4˝ finished Tulip units (see page 41).

3. Referring to the Quilt Assembly Diagram (opposite), arrange the (32) Quarter-HST units into 4 rows of 8 blocks each. Sew the blocks together and press the seams open.

4. Sew the corresponding borders to the left and right edges of Border 2 and press.

5. Sew a Tulip unit to the left and right edges of the remaining two borders, making sure that the Tulips are oriented correctly. Press the seams towards the Tulip units.

6. Sew the top and bottom borders to the corresponding edges of Border 3.

BORDER FOUR: 4″ wide

1. Make the strip sets as follows: Sew a 2″ × WOF Fabric E strip to both edges of each 1½″ × WOF Fabric H strip. Press the seams towards Fabric E. Trim all 4 strip sets to 4½″ × 40½″.

2. Sew a strip to the left and right edges of Border 3. Sew a 4½″ Fabric G square to the left and right edges of the remaining 2 strip sets and sew these borders to the top and bottom edges of Border 3.

BORDER FIVE: 6″ wide, swap in any 6″ finished block for the X Blocks

1. Using the Fabrics D, F and I, make (36) 6″ finished X Block units (see page 44).

2. Sew the X Block units into 2 Borders of 8 blocks each and 2 Borders of 10 blocks each.

3. Sew an 8-block Border to the left and anoher to the right edges of Border 4. Next, sew a 10-block Border to the top and another to the bottom edges of Border 4.

Finishing

1. Piece the backing to be at least 68″ × 68″.

2. Sandwich, baste and quilt as desired.

3. Square up the quilt and attach the 2½″ wide binding using your preferred method.

Quilt Assembly Diagram

Bluegrass

Finished Quilt Size: 84½″ × 84½″

Quilted by Crinklelove

While a medallion quilt border can be made from just one block, it doesn't have to be. I designed this quilt with mixing it up in mind. Different blocks and shapes are joined together to create interest and are broken up with bigger strips of fabric to make the design elements really shine.

The layout reminds me of a formal European garden with paths and new things to discover around every bend, but the fun prints of this quilt aren't fussy at all. Green is my favorite color and may have been more appropriate for a garden-inspired quilt, yet I couldn't resist using this fresh take on a classic color combination. Plus, in Kentucky, where I live, the grass is definitely blue.

MATERIALS

Fabric A: ¾ yard Orange print

Fabric B: 2½ yards Light Blue solid

Fabric C: 1⅜ yards Pink geometric

Fabric D: 1 yard low-volume White and Blue print

Fabric E: ⅜ yard Navy dot

Fabric F: ¼ yard Orange solid

Fabric G: ½ yard low-volume White and Orange print

Fabric H: 1 yard Navy print

Fabric I: ⅜ yard Orange plaid

Fabric J: ⅓ yard Navy and White floral

Fabric K: 1⅜ yards Orange floral

Backing Fabric: 7¾ yards

Binding Fabric: ¾ yard

Batting: 2½ yards, 90″ wide

> *The layout reminds me of a formal European garden with high hedges along narrow paths and new things to discover around every bend.*

CUTTING

Center Medallion

From Fabric A, cut:
- (1) 4½″ square

From Fabric B, cut:
- (4) 2½″ squares
- (4) 2½″ × 4½″ rectangles

From Fabric C, cut:
- (12) 2½″ squares
- (4) 2½″ × 4½″ rectangles

From Fabric D, cut:
- (4) 3″ squares
- (8) 2½″ squares

From Fabric E, cut:
- (4) 3″ squares

From Fabric F, cut:
- (4) 2½″ squares

Border 1

From Fabric G, cut:
- (12) 3½″ × 2½″ rectangles

From Fabric H, cut:
- (12) 3½″ squares

Border 2

From Fabric B, cut:
- (4) 2½″ × 3½″ rectangles
- (4) 2½″ × 5½″ rectangles

From Fabric D, cut:
- (8) 2½″ × 3½″ rectangles

From Fabric F, cut:
- (4) 2½″ squares

From Fabric J, cut:
- (8) 2½″ squares

Border 3

From Fabric G, cut:
- (4) 2½″ × 3½″ rectangles

From Fabric H, cut:
- (12) 3½″ squares

From Fabric I, cut:
- (8) 2½″ × 7½″ rectangles

Border 4

From Fabric D, cut:
- (8) 2½″ × 13½″ rectangles

From Fabric J, cut:
- (8) 2½″ squares

Border 5

From Fabric B, cut:
- (6) 2½″ × WOF
    - sub-cut into:
        - (96) 2½″ squares
- (2) 4½″ × WOF
    - sub-cut into:
        - (4) 4½″ × 8½″ rectangles
        - (4) 4½″ squares

From Fabric K, cut:
- (3) 4½″ × WOF
    - sub-cut into:
        - (24) 4½″ squares

Border 6

From Fabric C, cut:
- (4) 4½″ × 40½″ strips

From Fabric E, cut:
- (4) 4½″ squares

Border 7

From Fabric B, cut:
- (4) 2¾″ × WOF strips
    - sub-cut into:
        - (48) 2¾″ squares

From Fabric F, cut:
- (12) 2″ squares

From Fabric G, cut:
- (3) 2¾″ × WOF strips
    - sub-cut into:
        - (48) 2″ × 2¾″ rectangles

From Fabric H, cut:
- (8) 6½″ squares

From Fabric K, cut:
- (4) 6½″ × 24½″ strips

CUTTING, *continued*

Border 8

From Fabric D, cut:

(6) 3½″ × WOF strips
sub-cut into:
(12) 3½″ × 18½″ strips

From Fabric J, cut:

(12) 3½″ squares

Border 9

From Fabric A, cut:

(3) 6½″ × WOF strips
sub-cut into (16) 6½″
squares

From Fabric B, cut:

(8) 3½″ × WOF strips
sub-cut into:
(96) 3½″ squares

(2) 6½″ × WOF strips
sub-cut into:
(12) 6½″ squares

From Fabrics H and K, cut:

(8) 6½″ squares

From Fabric I, cut:

(4) 6½″ squares

Border 10

From Fabric C, cut:

(8) 3½″ × 38″ strips

From Fabric E, cut:

(8) 3½″ squares

Assembly

CENTER MEDALLION: 12″ square

1. Using the 4½″ Fabric A square and (4) 2½″ Fabric B squares, sew a 4″ finished Square-in-a-Square unit (see page 37).

2. Using (4) 2½″ × 4½″ Fabric B rectangles and (8) 2½″ Fabric C squares, sew (4) 2″ × 4″ finished Flying Geese units (see page 21).

3. Using (4) 2½″ × 4½″ Fabric C rectangles and (8) 2½″ Fabric D squares, sew (4) 2″ × 4″ finished Flying Geese units.

4. Sew a Fabric B/C Flying Geese unit to a Fabric C/D Flying Geese unit as indicated below.

Double Geese: Make 4

5. Using (4) 3″ Fabric D and (4) 3″ Fabric E squares, sew (8) 2″ finished Half-Square Triangle units (see page 20). Trim to 2½″ square if necessary.

6. Sew (1) Fabric D/E HST unit to each of (4) 2½″ Fabric C squares and (4) 2½″ Fabric F squares as indicated below. Arrange and sew the units together to form a 4-patch.

HST 4-patch: Make 4

7. Sew a double Flying Geese unit from Step 4 to the left and right sides of the Fabric A/B Square-in-a-Square unit to form the middle row of the center medallion.

8. Sew a 4-patch block from Step 6 to the left and right sides of the remaining two double Flying Geese units to form the top and bottom rows. Sew the top and bottom rows in place as indicated.

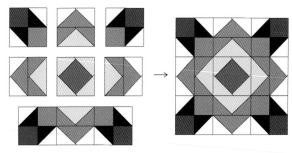

Medallion Assembly Diagram

BORDER ONE: 3˝ wide

1. Sew a 3½˝ Fabric H square to left and right edges of (4) 2½˝ × 3½˝ Fabric G rectangles. Sew a 2½˝ × 3½˝ Fabric G rectangle to the left and right edges of the 4 Fabric H/G units. Join a Border to the left and right sides of the center medallion. Press the seams towards the center.

2. Sew a 3½˝ Fabric H square to each end of the remaining 2 Borders. Press the seams towards Fabric H. Join a border to the top and bottom edges of the center medallion. Press the seams towards the center. Unless otherwise noted, press the seams toward the newly attached border throughout.

BORDER TWO: 2˝ wide

1. Sew a 2½˝ Fabric J square to each of (4) 2½˝ × 3½˝ Fabric B rectangles. Sew a 2½˝ × 3½˝ Fabric D rectangle to the left and right edges of (2) 2½˝ Fabric F squares. Attach a

Fabric J/B unit to the left and right edges of the Fabric D/F units. Join a border to the left and right edges of Border 1.

2. Sew a 2½˝ Fabric J square to each of (4) 2½˝ × 5½˝ Fabric B rectangles. Sew a 2½˝ × 3½˝ Fabric D rectangle to the left and right edges of (2) 2½˝ Fabric F squares. Attach a Fabric J/B unit to the left and right edges of the Fabric D/F units. Join a border to each the top and bottom edges of Border 1.

BORDER THREE: 3″ wide

1. Sew a 3½″ Fabric H square to the left and right edges of (4) 2½″ × 3½″ Fabric G rectangles. Sew a 2½″ × 7½″ Fabric I rectangle to the left and right edges of (4) Fabric H/G units. Join a border to the left and right edges of Border 2. Press the seams towards Border 2.

2. Sew a 3½″ Fabric H square to the left and right edges of the two remaining borders. Press the seams towards Fabric H. Join a border to the top and bottom edges of Border 2.

BORDER FOUR: 2″ wide

1. Sew a 2½″ × 13½″ Fabric D strip to the left and right edges of (4) 2½″ Fabric J squares. Join a border to the left and right edges of Border 3. Press the seams towards Border 4.

2. Sew a 2½″ Fabric J square to the left and right edges of the remaining two borders. Join a border to the top and bottom edges of Border 3.

BORDER FIVE: 4″ wide, swap in any 4″ finished block for the Square-in-a-Square blocks

1. Using (24) 4½″ Fabric K squares and (96) 2½″ Fabric B squares, construct (24) 4″ finished Square-in-a-Square units (see page 37). Sew the Square-in-a-Square units into 8 sets of 3.

2. Sew a set of 3 Square-in-a-Square units to the left and right edges of (4) 4½″ × 8½″ Fabric B rectangles. Join a border to the left and right edges of Border 4. Press the seams towards Border 4.

3. Sew a 4½″ Fabric B square to the left and right edges of the remaining 2 borders. Press the seams towards the Fabric B squares. Join a border to the top and bottom of Border 4.

Square-in-a-Square small border: Make 2

Square-in-a-Square large border: Make 2

BORDER SIX: 4″ wide

1. Join a 4½″ × 40½″ Fabric C strip to the left and right edges of Border 5. Press the seams towards Border 6.

2. Sew a 4½″ Fabric E square to each end of the remaining (2) 4½″ × 40½″ Fabric C strips. Press the seams towards Fabric C. Join a border to the top and bottom edges of Border 5.

BORDER SEVEN: 6″ wide, swap in any 6″ finished block for the Modified Plus blocks

1. Construct (12) 6″ finished Modified Plus blocks using (4) 2″ × 2¾″ Fabric G rectangles, (1) 2″ Fabric F square and (4) 2¾″ Fabric B squares per block. Arrange and sew into a 9-patch according to the diagram below.

Modified Plus Block: Make 12

2. Sew a 6½″ Fabric H square to the left and right edges of (4) 6½″ × 24½″ Fabric K strips. Sew a Modified Plus block to the left and right edges of the Fabric H/K units. Join a border to the left and right edges of Border 6. Press the seams towards Border 6.

3. Sew a Modified Plus block to the left and right of the remaining two borders. Join a border to the top and bottom edges of Border 6.

BORDER EIGHT: 3″ wide, swap in any 3″ block for the plain squares

1. Sew a 3½″ Fabric J square to the left and right edges of (4) 3½″ × 18½″ Fabric D strips. Sew a 3½″ × 18½″ Fabric D strip to the opposite edge of each Fabric J square to create 4 border sets. Join a set to the left and right edges of Border 7. Press the seams towards Border 8.

2. Sew a 3½″ Fabric J square to the left and right edges of the remaining 2 border sets. Press the seams towards Fabric D. Join an assembled border to the top and bottom edges of Border 7.

BORDER NINE: 6″ wide, swap in any 6″ finished block for the Square-in-a-Square blocks

1. Sew (1) 6½″ Fabric H square to the left and right of (4) 6½″ Fabric I squares. Sew a 6½″ Fabric B square to the left and right side of the units to form the center unit for each border.

2. Using (16) 6½″ Fabric A squares and (64) 3½″ Fabric B squares, construct (16) 6″ finished Square-in-a-Square units (see page 37).

3. Using (8) 6½″ Fabric K squares and (32) 3 ½″ Fabric B squares, construct (8) 6″ finished Square-in-a-Square units.

4. Sew the Square-in-a-Square units into 8 sets of 3. Sew a set of 3 to the left and right edges of each center unit constructed in Step 1. Join an assembled border to the left and right edges of Border 8. Press the seams towards Border 8.

5. Sew a 6½″ Fabric B square to the left and right edges of the remaining 2 borders. Join an assembled border to the top and bottom of Border 8.

1. Sew a 3½″ × 38″ Fabric C strip to the left and right edges of (4) 3½″ Fabric E squares. Press the seams towards Join an assembled border to the left and right edges of Border 9.

2. Sew a 3½″ Fabric E square to the left and right edges of the remaining 2 borders. Press the seams towards Fabric C. Join an assembled border to the top and bottom edges of Border 9.

Finishing

1. Piece the backing to be at least 92″ × 92″.

2. Sandwich, baste and quilt as desired.

3. Square up the quilt and attach the 2½″ wide binding using your preferred method.

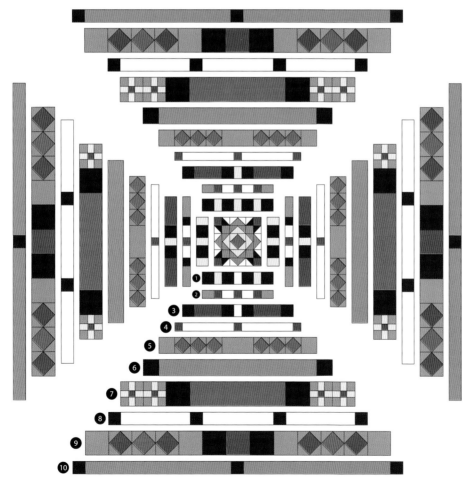

Quilt Assembly Diagram

Techniques

Appliqué

When it comes to appliqué, I love stitching my pieces by hand. I know that the needle-turn method is not for everyone so all of the appliquéd blocks in the book can also be done using fusible web as well. Both methods are easy and work well. Choose the one that is right for you.

NEEDLE-TURN APPLIQUÉ

There are a few different methods of needle-turn appliqué, I use Carolyn Friedlander's, as shown in her book, *Savor Each Stitch*.

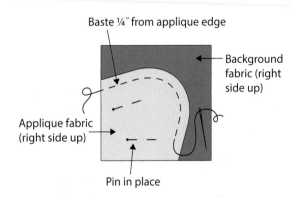

Baste ¼˝ from applique edge

Background fabric (right side up)

Applique fabric (right side up)

Pin in place

1. Pin the appliqué in place with appliqué pins. Using contrasting thread, hand (or machine) baste the appliqué panel to the background ¼˝ from the raw edge with long basting stitches. Remove the basting pins as you go.

2. Thread the appliqué needle with matching thread. Knot at one end. Fold the raw edge of the appliqué under to meet the basting stitch, creating a ⅛˝ turn-under allowance. Bring the threaded needle up through all the layers, close to the edge.

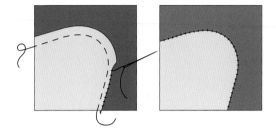

3. Continuing to fold the raw edge in to meet the basting stitch, direct the needle down through the background fabric at the folded appliqué edge (perpendicular to the appliqué edge) and back up through the appliqué panel ⅛˝ from the previous stitch.

4. Continue around the appliqué until all the edges are folded under and stitched down. Knot the threads at the back of the project.

5. After the appliqué is fully attached, remove the basting stitches and press flat.

FUSIBLE APPLIQUÉ

1. Trace the appliqué shape onto template plastic. Do NOT add a seam allowance. Cut your template from the plastic.

2. Following the manufacturers instructions, attach the fusible web to the wrong side of the appliqué. Trace the template onto the paper backing of the fusible web.

3. Cut out the shape along the traced lines and remove the paper backing. Position the shape on the base fabric and fuse in place.

4. Sew the shape in place along the raw edges using a small zig zag or other decorative stitch of your choosing.

Foundation Paper Piecing

1. Let's practice! Draw a 6½″ square on a piece of 20 lb. paper and center a 6″ square inside that. From the lower left corner of the inner square, draw 4 lines. Number each Section 1-5.

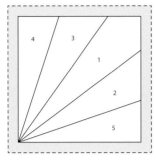

Practice Block

2. Beginning with Section 1, pin your fabric to the wrong side of the template, leaving at least ¼″ of fabric extending past the drawn lines. The right side of the fabric should be facing up.

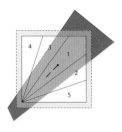 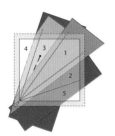

3. After ensuring that your fabric selection for Section 2 also has at least ¼″ around all sides (hold the layers up to a sunny window to check), place the fabric for Section 2 on top of the fabric for Section 1, right sides together. Pin in place. Flip over so that the template numbers are facing you and the fabric is on the bottom.

4. Set your machine's stitch length to 1.8 mm. This will make removing the template paper a lot easier. Sew along the line between Sections 1 and 2, extending into the seam allowance.

5. Fold the paper along the sewn line so that the right sides of the paper are facing. Measure ¼″ away from the sewn line onto the exposed fabric. Trim away the excess fabric and press the seams to one side.

6. Repeat for all the sections of the template, working in numerical order (Fig. 5) and press all the seams again, this time on the right side of the fabric.

7. With the paper side facing up, trim around the template. Make sure to include any marked seam allowances.

Using Templates

You will find that a number of the components in this book rely on special templates for their construction. Here are some tips to help in making the use of these templates easy.

1. Review the markings on each individual template before using it. If a template needs to be enlarged, copy it at the appropriate percentage. Likewise, if the template requires you to add a seam allowance, do that after any enlarging or reducing.

2. Trace your template in one of two ways:

    a. Place a piece of template plastic over the template and trace the cutting lines and any other additional markings with a fine tipped permanent marker. OR...

    b. Place a piece of card stock over the template and trace the cutting lines and any other markings using a pencil. If you have trouble seeing the lines, tape the template and the card stock to a sunny window.

3. Cut your template out, then place template right side up on your fabric. Using a marking pen, trace around it. Transfer any necessary markings to the fabric as well. Take care to test your marking tool on a piece of scrap fabric to determine whether the marks will be visible.

4. Cut the fabric along the marked lines.

Templates & Patterns

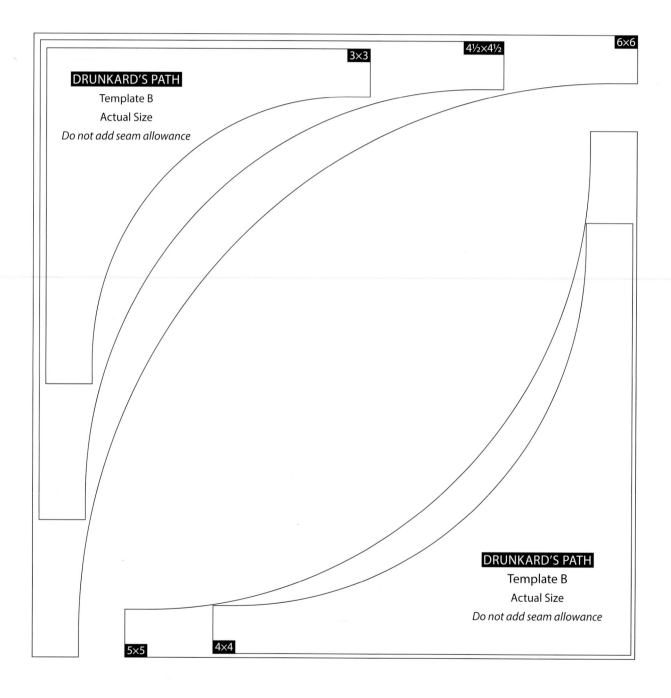

DRUNKARD'S PATH

Template B

Actual Size

Do not add seam allowance

3×3

4½×4½

6×6

5×5

4×4

DRUNKARD'S PATH

Template B

Actual Size

Do not add seam allowance

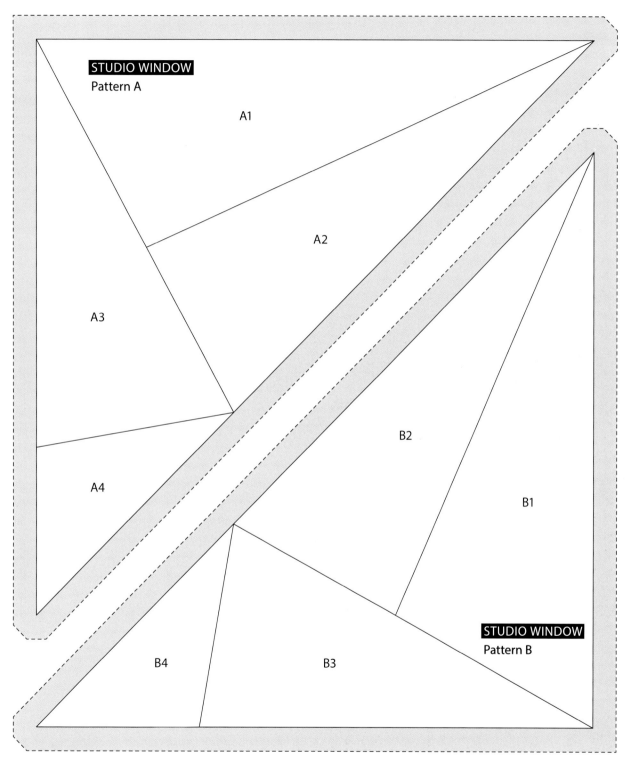

STUDIO WINDOW
Pattern A

A1

A2

A3

A4

B2

B1

STUDIO WINDOW
Pattern B

B4

B3

Actual Size

- - - cut line

—— stitch line

seam allowance

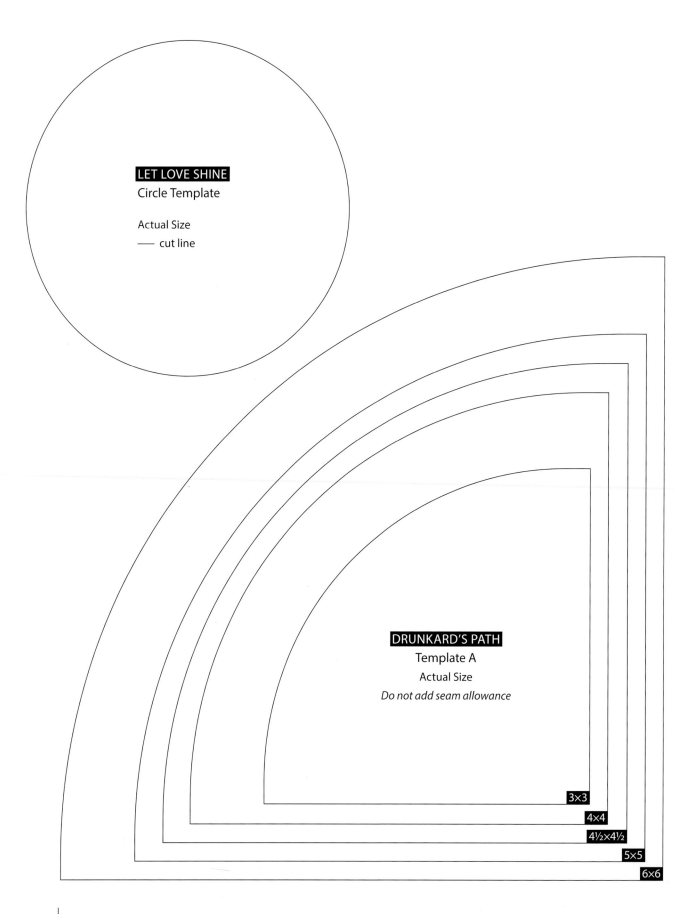

LET LOVE SHINE
Circle Template

Actual Size
—— cut line

DRUNKARD'S PATH
Template A
Actual Size
Do not add seam allowance

3×3
4×4
4½×4½
5×5
6×6

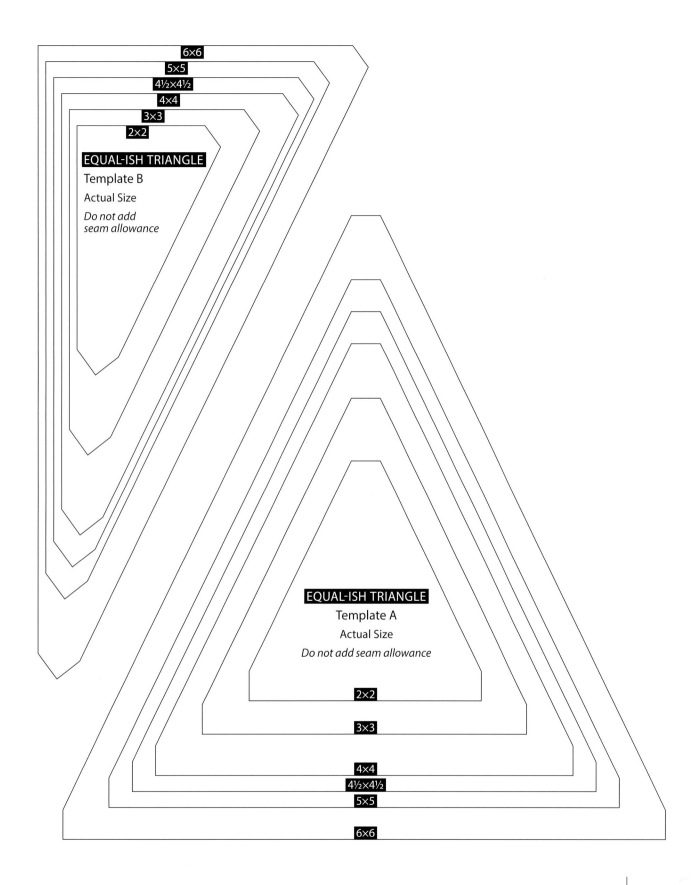

EQUAL-ISH TRIANGLE

Template B

Actual Size

Do not add seam allowance

6×6
5×5
4½×4½
4×4
3×3
2×2

EQUAL-ISH TRIANGLE

Template A

Actual Size

Do not add seam allowance

2×2
3×3
4×4
4½×4½
5×5
6×6

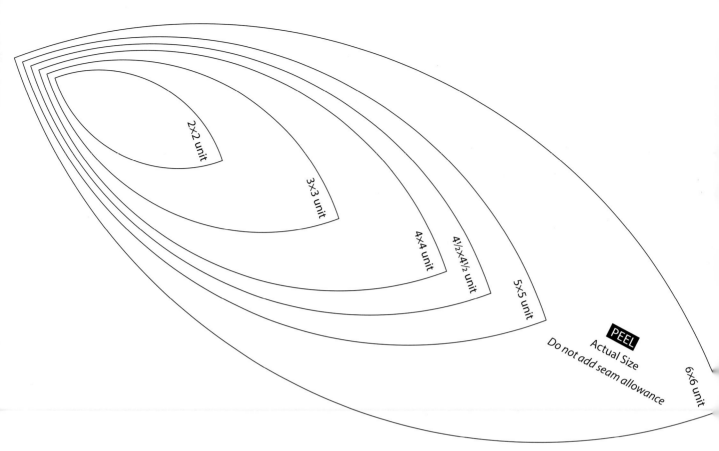

2×2 unit

3×3 unit

4×4 unit

4½×4½ unit

5×5 unit

PEEL
Actual Size
Do not add seam allowance

6×6 unit

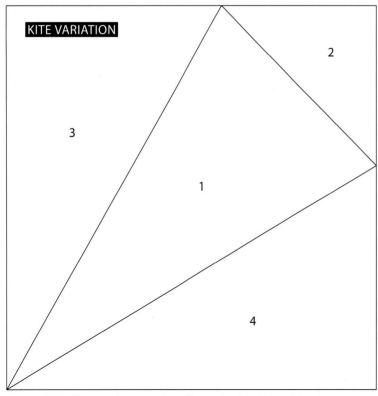

KITE VARIATION

2

3

1

4

Add ¼" seam allowance to entire perimeter during trimming.

Photocopy Sizing Chart

BLOCK UNITS		
6×6	enlarge 150%
5×5	enlarge 125%
4½×4½	enlarge 112.5%
4×4	100%
3×3	reduce 75%
2×2	reduce 50%

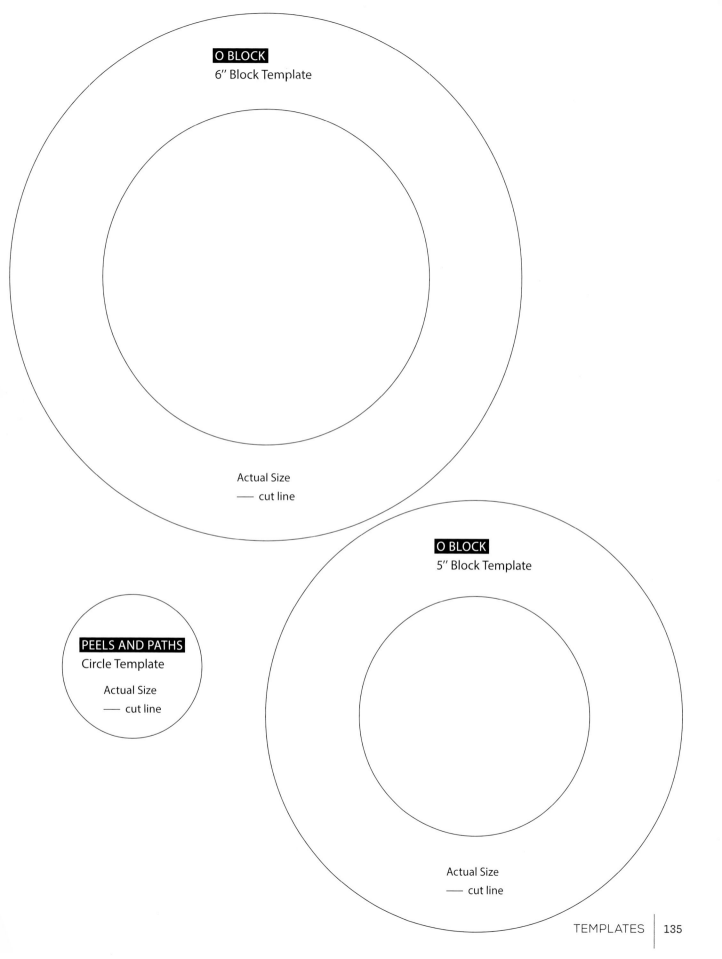

O BLOCK
6" Block Template

Actual Size
—— cut line

O BLOCK
5" Block Template

Actual Size
—— cut line

PEELS AND PATHS
Circle Template

Actual Size
—— cut line

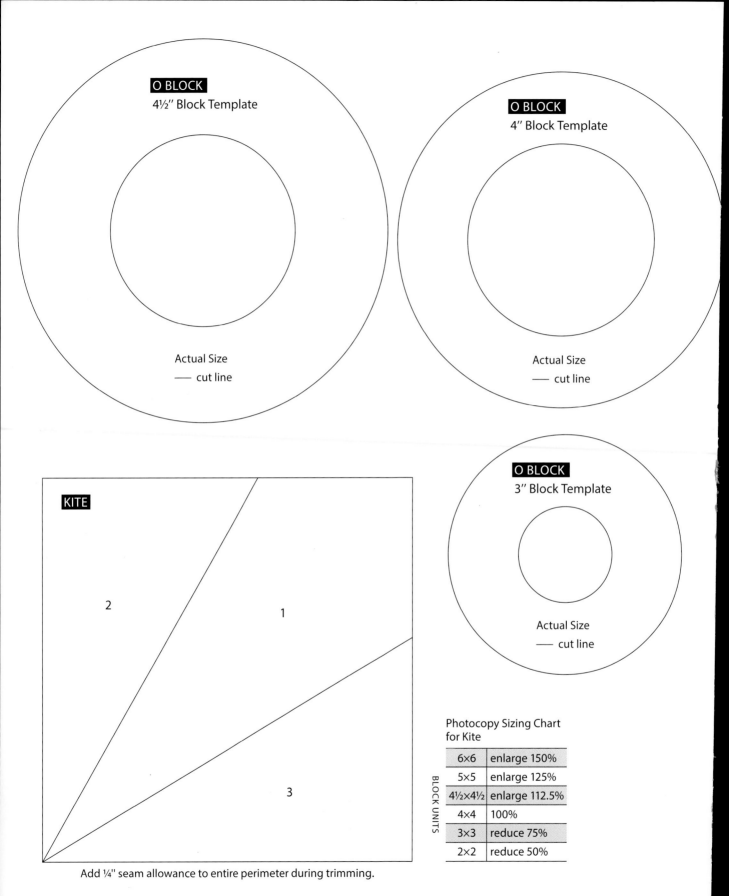

O BLOCK
4½″ Block Template

Actual Size
—— cut line

O BLOCK
4″ Block Template

Actual Size
—— cut line

O BLOCK
3″ Block Template

Actual Size
—— cut line

KITE

2

1

3

Add ¼″ seam allowance to entire perimeter during trimming.

Photocopy Sizing Chart for Kite

BLOCK UNITS	
6×6	enlarge 150%
5×5	enlarge 125%
4½×4½	enlarge 112.5%
4×4	100%
3×3	reduce 75%
2×2	reduce 50%

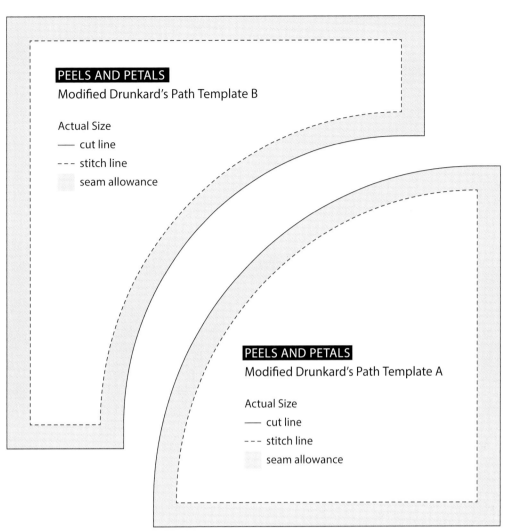

PEELS AND PETALS
Modified Drunkard's Path Template B

Actual Size
—— cut line
- - - stitch line
▨ seam allowance

PEELS AND PETALS
Modified Drunkard's Path Template A

Actual Size
—— cut line
- - - stitch line
▨ seam allowance

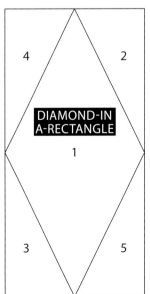

Add ¼˝ seam allowance to entire perimeter during trimming.

Photocopy Sizing Chart
for Diamond in a Rectangle

BLOCK UNITS		
3 × 6	enlarge 200%
2½ × 5	enlarge 167%
2 × 4	enlarge 133%
1½ × 3	100%

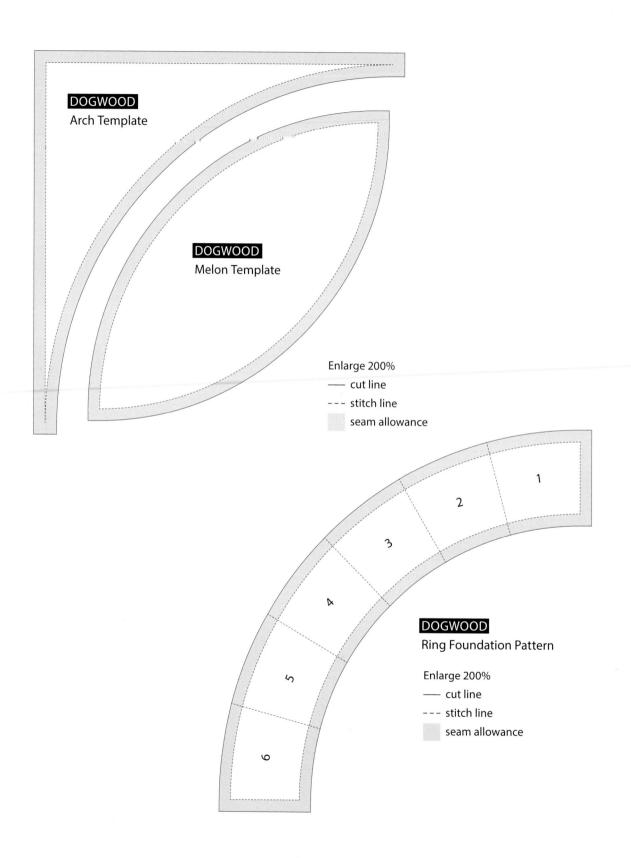

DOGWOOD
Arch Template

DOGWOOD
Melon Template

Enlarge 200%
—— cut line
‑‑‑ stitch line
■ seam allowance

DOGWOOD
Ring Foundation Pattern

Enlarge 200%
—— cut line
‑‑‑ stitch line
■ seam allowance

1
2
3
4
5
6

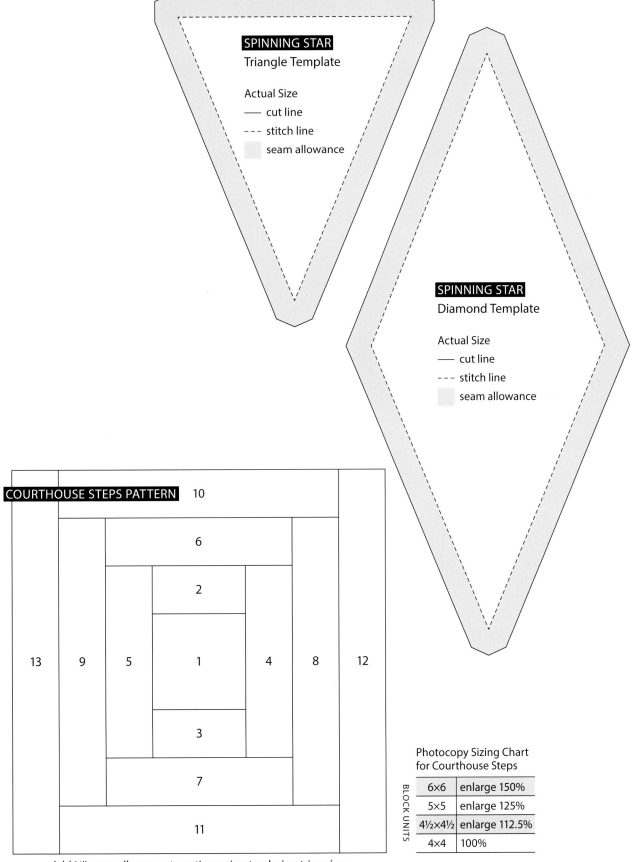

SPINNING STAR
Triangle Template

Actual Size
— cut line
- - - stitch line
seam allowance

SPINNING STAR
Diamond Template

Actual Size
— cut line
- - - stitch line
seam allowance

COURTHOUSE STEPS PATTERN

			10				
			6				
			2				
13	9	5	1	4	8	12
			3				
			7				
			11				

Add ¼" seam allowance to entire perimeter during trimming.

Photocopy Sizing Chart
for Courthouse Steps

BLOCK UNITS		
6×6	enlarge 150%
5×5	enlarge 125%
4½×4½	enlarge 112.5%
4×4	100%

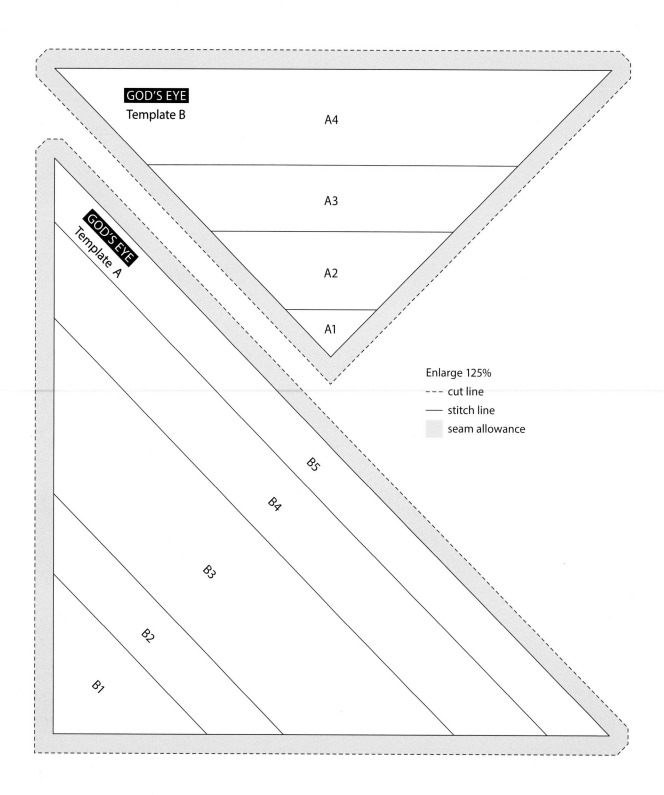

GOD'S EYE
Template B

A4

A3

A2

A1

GOD'S EYE
Template A

B5

B4

B3

B2

B1

Enlarge 125%
- - - cut line
—— stitch line
▨ seam allowance

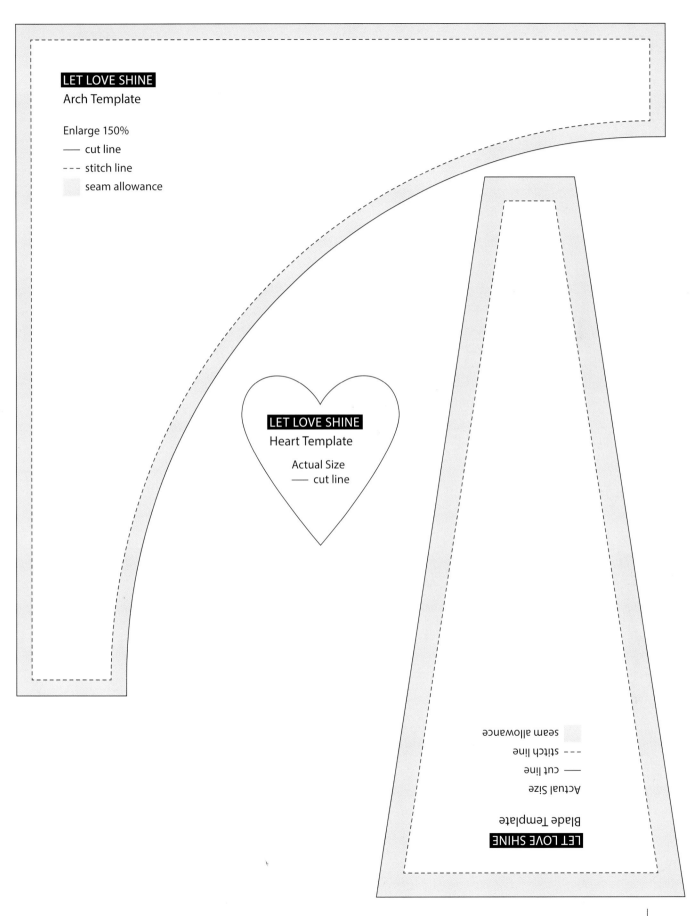

LET LOVE SHINE
Arch Template

Enlarge 150%
—— cut line
- - - stitch line
  seam allowance

LET LOVE SHINE
Heart Template

Actual Size
—— cut line

LET LOVE SHINE
Blade Template

Actual Size
—— cut line
- - - stitch line
  seam allowance

Acknowledgements

Susanne Woods and her unwavering belief in me and my idea made this book a reality. I am grateful that she did not give up on this project even when we both thought that was the smart thing to do. This book is better for her persistence, input, guidance and friendship. Thank you, Susanne.

The entire Lucky Spool Media team was a joy to work with and made my job easy. Special thanks to: Kari Vojtechovsky and Courtney Kyle for understanding just what the illustrations needed to look like; Nissa Brehmer for the gorgeous photography; Kristy Zacharias for working hard to make my vision for the design even better in reality than I could have hoped; and Shea Henderson for double- and triple-checking all the little details and math. I appreciate all of your hard work on my behalf.

I am lucky to have good and talented friends in my corner. Marcia Seiler read my contracts and took my photo without hesitation. She also made me look good in the process. Sarah Cosper and Melissa Mortenson stepped in to cut fabric and sew blocks when I was

short on time. Darcy Childress, Jill Evans and Melissa Frantz were quick to respond to my random questions texts and provided input without realizing it. Emily Demsky and Caroline Thornewill answered my calls, listened and encouraged me throughout this entire project. Thank you all for your invaluable help.

A huge shout out to my daughters, Jane and Kate, for being my biggest cheerleaders. They are good sports, getting excited (or at least pretending to) when I show them something, helping without being asked (most of the time) and turning down the music when I need silence to think (which is often). You two are the best!

The largest measure of my thanks belongs to my husband. Thank you, Fatty, for being a great partner and my best friend. Your steadfast love, support and encouragement of my creative endeavors is an incredible blessing. I appreciate your willingness to shop alongside me for fabric and yarn and your understanding that I need a stash of both. I couldn't do any of it without you and feel incredibly lucky that we get to do life together.